Reimagining

WORK

From Suffering at Work to Creating a
More Loving, Compassionate, Abundant,
and Spiritually Aligned Life

Gissele Damiani-Taraba, MSc., MSW

Copyright

First edition: April 2023

ISBN: ISBN 978-1-7388531-0-6 (soft cover)
ISBN: ISBN 978-1-7388531-1-3 (e-book)
ISBN: ISBN 978-1-7388531-2-0 (audio)

Published by Gissele Damiani-Taraba, Maitri Centre

TABLE OF CONTENTS

Welcome! viii

Chapter 1 A New Beginning...1

    The need to reimagine work 4

Chapter 2 Where Do Our Ideas about Work Come From? 11

    My story 12

    9 to 5, 5 days a week, 365 days a year? 15

Chapter 3 How Our Consciousness Shapes Our Experiences at Work . 24

    What is real?... 25

    Consciousness and reality 28

Chapter 4 Living in the Flow 32

    Living and working from the flow.. 33

    Manifesting my "dream" job 34

    Tapping into our passions 36

    Redefining wealth.. 37

    Energy is the new currency 39

    Aligning with our abundance 40

Chapter 5 Discovering Compassion 48

    Defining compassion 48

    The myth of tough love 51

    The myth of professionalism... 54

    The myth of weakness and vulnerability....................................... 56

    The myth of narcissism 58

Chapter 6 Compassion for Myself... 60

    Compassion turned inward 61

    This isn't about them. It's about you. 63

Practicing self-love and self-compassion.....................................65

Compassion's unexpected impact 71

Regret...72

Chapter 7 Compassion for Others **75**

We are interconnected..75

The walls of separation...79

Hierarchy of compassion..83

Punishment as a deterrent 86

Chapter 8 A Return to Ourselves.. **88**

Reimagining others 89

Chapter 9 Redefining Power and Strength......................... **99**

Trust and courage 101

The power of presence...104

Doing versus being 106

The transformative power of love 109

Chapter 10 Changing Our Consciousness to Change Our Work and Our Lives.. **111**

Start where you are..111

Acknowledging our identities 113

What do I need? 119

Mindfully dealing with negative thoughts..................................121

The cost of not changing...124

Chapter 11 Taking Our Power Back **125**

No one is coming to save you 126

What do you want?...127

Our attachment to fear..129

Reimagining my reality, at work 131

Chapter 12 Releasing Resistance.. **136**

Resistance 138

The need to be great!.. 140

Stuck in the victim story 144

CRISIS environments.. 145

Drama mama.. 146

Shame 148

Chapter 13 Workplace Leadership **154**

Treating our employees with compassion........................ 156

Fear versus empowerment.. 158

Power and workplace leadership...................................... 160

Buying into others' stories.. 161

The energy of nonprofits 163

Chapter 14 When Things Go "Wrong" **167**

What happened to forgiveness at work? 168

Making mistakes 171

Living in the energy of our values.................................... 173

Difficult conversations.. 175

Terminating someone with compassion 181

Chapter 15 When Life Gives Us a Push **185**

Transforming seeming negatives into positives 186

Reframing failure 188

Receiving a work plan.. 190

Chapter 16 Addressing Toxicity with Compassion............ **192**

Making judgments.. 193

Reimagining how we deal with bullying.......................... 195

Victims or oppressors? 199

Dealing with racism with compassion............................ 201

Chapter 17 Opening Up to Magic **207**

Deserving my magical life 208

You have to be out of your mind. 210

The heart always knows. 212

Aligning with our desires...213

Why it's important to live our dreams 216

Believe in your vision more than your reality. 218

Gratitude and joy as cheat codes..222

Epilogue **228**

Acknowledgments **230**

Notes **232**

About the Author **241**

Welcome!

I'm so grateful for your interest in reading this book and joining me in my journey to rediscovering work. My greatest desire is that this book is of assistance to you on your journey. The strength of this book lies in its application and practice, not solely its knowledge. You have the power to change your life right now; you just need to choose to do whatever it takes to make that shift. I want you to take what I've said in this book and try it out for yourselves.

The framework for this book will follow the pattern of sharing my experiences to expand your awareness. Questions are embedded through heart stretches to uplevel your practices and challenge you to change how you respond to events and interactions in your personal lives and at work. Over time, as you practice self-compassion and self-love, love and compassion will be your default setting. This is embodiment, where you become the person you want to be in every aspect of your life and with every being you meet.

Much love to you always,

Gissele

Chapter 1

A New Beginning

Pain pushes until vision pulls.
~ Michael Beckwith

I was frustrated. I'd left my employment two years earlier to fulfill my dream of spreading love and compassion at home and work, but I was making little progress. I'd been busting my butt producing content—social media, a podcast, a blog—paying for marketing, and going on podcast shows to promote my work . . . and nothing. Not a thing. Even though everyone told me how needed this was in our current world. I was particularly frustrated because I was in uncharted territory.

I'd always been an overachiever. I have two master's degrees, had risen to leadership positions in organizations, and had managed millions of dollars in business even while young. But here I was, putting in maximum effort with minimal progress. I was venting to my husband, David, asking him for his sage perspective on my new situation. He reassured me that it was all part of the journey and that everything would work out well.

But I was nervous. I hadn't been without income since I was thirteen years old.

"If you are THAT nervous," he said, shrugging, "why don't you get a job?"

In his mind, there was no need to suffer. Just make a choice about what you want to do because there are always options. And it wasn't like he suggested I return to a full-time permanent position. I could have gotten a contract or taken on part-time work as I grew my business. But his answer hit a nerve with me.

"Doesn't he believe in my abilities?" I asked myself. "Doesn't he believe I can succeed?"

I'd known David for over fifteen years. I knew that he believed in me. He has always supported me, and rather than be upset or afraid, he was happy for me when I left my high-paying but stressful job to pursue my dream.

Having practiced meditation for a long time and knowing the incredible power of my own inner wisdom, I knew the answer was within me. My husband was giving me a gift—I just couldn't see it. I sat down on my favorite office chair, took a deep breath, and went inward to understand why I was reacting to my husband's comment. Then it hit me.

"I don't want to get a job," I said to myself.

This answer surprised me. I'd been working since I was young. From babysitting at thirteen, to working at a daycare at sixteen, to working retail, then being a researcher in a hospital, then a Quality Assurance Manager, then finally rising to the position of Director at a Children's Aid Society, I was always employed somewhere, and I was always successful. So, what was the real issue?

And as I dove deeper into my own awareness, I heard myself say: "I don't like the way we 'work.'"

Throughout my professional career, I've experienced controlling bosses, takeovers and acquisitions, overwork, government oversight, bankruptcy, high-stress environments, lack of flexibility and trust, and the assignment of tasks that I didn't want to do. There were also relationship issues at work as well as unaddressed racism, discrimination, bullying, and harassment. The thought of having to check in with people and tell someone where I was going all the time out of fear that they'd think I wasn't working didn't appeal to me. It also didn't appeal to me to go back to working nine to five, Monday to Friday, as I was enjoying being there for my children when they needed me.

At first, I thought that my desire not to work was lazy, but I knew there was more to these feelings. I love to be of service, and I love creating things, so it wasn't about my not working per se. In fact, the more I contemplated going back to work, the more I understood that the way we "work" doesn't always align with our souls. Perhaps this is why so many people dread Mondays. If our work felt aligned, there would be no dread. We would all be eager to work on projects that excited our passions and aligned with who we are. As I reflected on the type of workplaces I'd want to return to, I realized I desired to bring more of my true self into work. And if I didn't wish to return to a work environment that didn't honor my true self, then I wouldn't want to create a similar one for my staff if I had them.

I began to reimagine how I and others work. I dreamed of seeing companies where people came together in joy, fun, and alignment, working together on a shared vision and for mutual benefit. I dreamed of seeing people earn more than just a living wage and truly flourishing. I wish that all people could have a positive work-life balance, joy, prosperity, and community.

"A company is not family," someone once said to me in response to my desire to change how I and others work.

"You're right. Families can be dysfunctional," I replied, laughing. I wanted to create a compassionate and loving, joyful community at work.

The need to reimagine work

Workplaces are changing at a rapid pace, so rapidly that leaders are struggling with staffing levels and worker engagement. When the COVID-19 virus made its way onto the scene, at least 43 per cent of organizations were forced to shut down, leaving many businesses struggling to stay afloat.[1] Those that did survive the transition accomplished this with varying levels of success. During this time, I was asked by a few business owner friends what they could do to make their workplaces more resilient. My answer was and still is that we must change the way we view work.

The Great Resignation gave us the first indication that not all was right within workplaces. Flocks of people quit their jobs and started their own businesses or decided to switch workplaces. It has been estimated that in the United States, about 47.4 million people voluntarily left their jobs for better work during the pandemic, which is 4.3 million more than during 2019.[2] In Canada, an estimated 24 per cent of the workforce left their current role or position in 2022.[3] One thing that has become clear to me is that people are no longer interested in working in environments where they're not treated with care. In fact, "not being respected" was the third highest reason why the majority of US workers left their jobs in 2021.[4] The top two reasons were not enough compensation and lack of opportunities.

Toxic work environments are no longer being accepted as the "way things are around here."[5] Employees want these issues addressed and managed by their leaders; a toxic culture is more than ten times more likely to contribute to attrition than compensation.[6] People no longer tolerate being seen as "cogs" in a wheel or as replaceable, disposable widgets.

The shifts we see also reflect a desire for workplaces that pay living wages, give employees benefits that support their families comfortably, and care about them as people. Workers also need proper resources to support their mental health.[7] They desire workplaces that motivate their soul with vision and direction.[8]

Living wages means paying people in a way that aligns with inflation and the cost of living. The rhetoric I've heard from some business owners is that they can't afford to provide staff with living wages. Often my answer is that maybe they can't afford to have a business. If the business is starting out, it's not possible to offer everyone higher wages. The owners may not even be taking wages themselves. However, there are ways of compensating staff in a way that honors people's time. They can offer equity in the business, greater time flexibility, and so much more. The key part here is that leaders and business owners have to believe they can thrive and be abundant *and* support the abundance of their staff. The two are not mutually exclusive, as we once were made to believe.

But increasing income is only part of the answer in ensuring employees flourish at work.

In response to a large number of people leaving their organization, a workplace leader once asked me, "Do you believe that if we raise the wages and give more benefits, people will stay?" My answer at the time was "maybe."

People's reasons for staying at a workplace long term are not solely motivated by money. Many leaders still underestimate the impact that culture has on the willingness to stay in an organization. I have personally observed excellent employees leave organizations because of a poor leadership style, not because of the nature or difficulty of the work or the pay.

The good news is that when I integrated compassion, love, flexibility, and vision within the departments I managed, people were excited about what they did and put their heart and soul into it; they were fueled by their passion, vision, and a desire to improve their workplaces. People were also kinder to one another and to themselves. Throughout my work career, I'd taken departments that were considered the "worst departments with the worst culture." But I knew the truth. I knew that those departments were made up of amazing people who wanted to be seen, heard, and valued and given the resources to enable them to do the best job they could.

There are many examples of the impact of compassion on workplace culture in the literature.[9] But without the willingness of leaders and staff to change, to see things differently, to alter how we perceive work beyond the nine to five, Monday to Friday grind, no strategies will lead to long-term business survival in the traditional sense. The future of work will continue to be fraught with volatility. "You can't put the toothpaste back in the tube," as my friend Jill would constantly say. Going back to the way we "worked" before the pandemic is no longer an option. In addition to the Great Resignation, approximately 50 per cent of the US workforce, according to a Gallup poll, are quiet quitting.[10] Quiet quitting has been defined as workers only doing what's in their job description and nothing more. When I was in the workplace, I personally experienced and observed others being expected to go above and beyond their workload. This additional work, which was usually the result of great performance, was often added without compensation. The quiet quitting phenomenon is our second indication that things are not alright at work.

People want to enjoy their workplaces and get paid to play. What does this mean? They desire to do what they love and get paid well while doing it. They don't want working on their passion to feel like work.[11] It's fascinating to me to observe that young people don't carry the same guilt and shame that some baby boomers and Generation Xers had, which was passed down from previous generations. The Millennial and Gen Z workforce does not share the perspective that we have to "earn" our wages by hating what we do. The previous World Wars forced our grandparents to do what they had to do rather than what they wanted to do. The Millennial and Gen Z workforce generation no longer feels this way.[12] Why?

Currently, in Canada, having a job doesn't guarantee you can afford a mortgage.[13] The rise in salaries has not yet caught up with the rise in the cost of living so people have to get creative in overcoming financial challenges. There is also low job security.[14] Recently, despite staffing shortages, large corporations have been laying off many employees.[15] Long gone are the days where one job could sustain you and your family long term.

Additionally, people are observing others make a lot of money doing things they enjoy, such as TikTok videos, YouTube shorts, and more.[16] I believe the rise of nonfungible tokens (NFTs), blockchain technology, passive income creation, and the creator economy will lead to a more equitable distribution of income.

"Young people are just lazy," I heard an older leader say to me, but I have not observed this in my numerous conversations with young people in the community. Today's youth see opportunity everywhere. They see that their videos can reach people worldwide. New careers are appearing, such as social media coordinators and TikTok managers.[17] The world is ripe with opportunity, so young people feel they have choices.

I also believe young people look at success differently. Just as some were forced to face life and death during the pandemic, many people started to question whether risking their lives for a job they didn't love or even like was worth it. That awareness has provoked the need to redefine prosperity and re-examine what it means to be abundant.[18]

Changing the way we work is also about incorporating key aspects of our personal lives into our professional lives. I no longer see work as separate from my personal life. Among my business friends, I see a desire to include spirituality at work or in business. This does not necessarily mean bringing crystals to work, although there's nothing wrong with this. I also don't mean religious practices. What I mean is that people are looking for more soul-based, heart-centered work, not merely profit-driven work.[19] I'm observing the desire to create with ease and grace, to align to their abundance and allow it to flow through inspired action rather than "earn it" through the grind. They are also looking to do good *and* make good pay.

This book is meant to help people make the most of their workplace experience and their personal life and to assist them in creating spaces that are compassionate, loving, joyful, flourishing, and meaningful. I also hope to encourage leaders in creating cultures of caring and community for mutual benefit and growth.

*♥ **Heart Stretch**: Close your eyes, and relax your entire body, beginning from the bottom of your feet all the way to the top of your head. Breathe in and out three times to keep your attention on your body. Now focus on your heart and rest your hand there. From this place, answer these questions:*

- *What impact did COVID-19 have on the way you work? Did it change how you work on a surface level, or did it completely change how you do your work?*
- *Did COVID-19 change how you feel about work?*

Chapter 2

Where Do Our Ideas about Work Come From?

What you think, you become.
What you feel, you attract.
What you imagine, you create.
~ Buddha

I was having a cup of tea, reflecting on the many stories I'd heard from my friends about their experiences in the workplace, and it occurred to me how often, at least in my generation, people were not living their dreams. Growing up, David dreamed of being an airplane pilot but settled for a well-paying job in the construction field. My sister didn't fulfill her dream of becoming a nurse until much later in life because she was strongly encouraged to acquire a more "profitable" degree. A number of my friends were also convinced by loved ones to choose specific careers that were deemed more socially acceptable. In fact, in Peru, everyone I knew was an engineer. How many of those people dreamed of being an engineer? As I dove deeper into my own beliefs about work, I wondered where all these ideas came from. Why is it that work currently looks the way it does?

For us to reimagine work, we must examine the factors that have led us to work the way we do. I'm not interested in the history of work so much as the thoughts and feelings that we have agreed to, as a collective consciousness or humanity, which dictate how we spend most of our lives. To understand how I ended up working in the places I did, I began by reflecting on my beliefs about workplace and career.

My story

I was born in Lima, Peru, and my family immigrated to Canada in the 1980s. The political, social, and economic situation in South America, according to my parents, was constantly oscillating from bad to worse. My parents worried about the effect of the economic and political instability on their hard-earned money.

Both my parents had grown up facing varying levels of poverty and instability and had worked since they were young. They were constantly saving money wherever they could. My mother is a gifted penny pincher and can turn two cents into a dollar. My father, who I believe always had the heart of an explorer, sought a place where our family could live and thrive without fear. Eventually, after a number of false starts, we immigrated to Canada following the "American/Canadian dream." To say the immigration journey was challenging for my parents is an understatement. The immigration process was expensive, and they had to have at least $20,000 in the bank to qualify for admission into Canada. Though both my parents were professionals in Peru, they came to Canada not knowing much

English, so they had to work multiple menial jobs as they became more familiar with the language. My dad held up to three jobs at one point while my mother worked at a factory where she hurt her back doing manual labor. Both went to night school when they could. Since my parents are both dark-skinned people, with accents, they faced discrimination and racism, especially at work.

Over time, and with much effort, things began to turn around for my mom and dad. My mom became employed at a bank, which offered her some job security. I wonder now if my mother chose to work in a bank to keep money up close. My father worked first contract and then full-time for Dupont until his retirement. Both taught me the value of working hard and trying your best. They also taught me that getting an education was pivotal to success. My parents attended university, but I'm unsure if either of them finished. Growing up, I never heard either say that they had their dream job or that it was even important to love what you did. Only recently have I learned that my mother dreamed of being a pharmacist and my father of being a fighter pilot. My mother couldn't afford schooling, and my dad had bad eyes, so he couldn't be a pilot. I wonder what my parents' lives would have been like had they lived their dreams.

Unfortunately, both my parents settled, like many people who don't realize they have other options. Even though my mother often complained about the treatment she received at work, she didn't change jobs mostly out of fear that she couldn't find something else or that her situation could somehow get worse. I don't remember ever hearing my dad speak about whether he had new dreams. I know that my mother always felt she had to sacrifice in order to earn everything she received.

I vividly remember the difficult times we experienced when my dad experienced layoffs. My parents kept my sister and I protected, but the stress of our financial instability wore my parents down and caused friction in their relationship. The messages I received from my parents were that it was important to have job security, to work hard to achieve success, to get the highest education possible to give you choices, and to do "whatever you need to do" to make it. This was what I perceived to be the immigrant mentality.

My parents believed they could trust only themselves to provide for the family. My mom and dad learned from their parents and ancestors before them that the world was a scary place, riddled with lack, and that resources were scarce, so to get yours, you had to compete with other people. In my community, there were no messages about making it "together." As my dad and I chatted about our family tree, I learned that my grandparents and their parents before them lived through death or abandonment, abuse and neglect, wars, drought, famine, and the Spanish Flu. They observed death and lack everywhere and lived their lives in fear. Thus, they imparted to their children a survival mentality that seemed to continue into the present.

Living and working from a state of fear is taxing to the body and to the mind. It is also not in alignment with the soul. When challenging circumstances come up, a state of arousal can motivate us to action, but for far too long, we have lived in anticipatory fear. As human beings, we were not meant to be in a constant state of arousal every minute of every day. This has impacted not only our personal lives but also how we achieve our goals through work. Our bodies and minds are tired of living this way. As a result, many people are burned out at work.

> ♥ *Heart Stretch: Close your eyes and relax your entire body beginning from the bottom of your feet all the way to the top of your head. Breathe in and out three times to keep your attention on your body. Now focus on your heart and rest your hand there. From this place, review your family history with work:*
>
> - *What stories did you learn from your parents about work?*
> - *How did your parents feel about their jobs? Were they living their dreams?*
> - *Did your parents tell you that living your dreams was important?*
> - *Did your parents tell you to focus on a specific profession? Why do you think that is?*
> - *Did these stories come from a place of love or fear?*

9 to 5, 5 days a week, 365 days a year?

It behooves us to examine how, as a society, we got to the point where most of us work nine to five, five days a week, most of the year. According to the *Online Etymology Dictionary,* in Old English, the word "work" means "something done, a discrete act performed by someone." However, its roots come from German and old Saxon meaning "to do" in the sense of physical effort, or exertion," which is why work is also sometimes called labor. The term working class is akin to the word laborers, although even those working in the corporate world could be classified under this category too.

Additionally, the word "business" is derived from the word "busy" and the suffix "ness." Interestingly, the word business also means "anxiety" in Old English. As a collective consciousness, we have aligned to being busy and viewing work as something that we force ourselves to do rather than focusing on the joy of creating. Keeping busy also keeps us distracted from the healing and growth we could do individually and as a species.

We have built a society where doing is more important than being. Relaxing or taking time to do nothing seems like sheer laziness, and often, we derive our value from how much we accomplish. Don't believe me? How many of us take pleasure in telling others just how busy we are? It's almost as if we're saying, "Look how important I am that I am so busy."

♥ Heart Stretch: Close your eyes and relax your entire body beginning from the bottom of your feet all the way to the top of your head. Breathe in and out three times to keep your attention on your body. Now focus on your heart and rest your hand there. From this place, reflect on your relationship with busyness:

- *What relationship does busyness have to power and authority?*
- *How important do you believe being busy is?*

Reimagining Work

A 2013 *Guardian* article claims that the word "work" has its history in punishment rather than support.[1] The author points out that the French word "travail" or in Spanish, "trabajo," is derived from the Latin word "tripaliare," which comes from "tripalium," meaning three sticks. Thus, the word "work" has its roots in torture or inflicting suffering. When we're doing work that isn't in alignment with who we are, it can certainly feel like torture!

The article offered me two key insights. First, the way we work does not make us feel free. All our toiling has not freed us from poverty. In fact, the cost of living is even higher, so people now feel like they have to work more. Second, we don't feel like we have choices. We are trapped by our relationship with work. Given these beliefs, it's no wonder our perspective on work is so challenging.

When did we decide that we were created solely to work? When did we as a collective decide to spend our whole lives doing a job we might or might not like so that we could eventually retire and then start to live? Why do we defer our happiness to some future that may never come? Some people even struggle with retirement as they so thoroughly identify with their identity as "workers" or "leaders."

Several European countries are now choosing to work four days a week,[2] but I'm not sure this will address our unhealthy perspective on work. For the most part, work tends to look the same worldwide. Workplaces tend to be hierarchical and separate from our personal lives and many workers have poor work-life balance. We punch in, do something nine to five, and then leave the weekend for personal matters. Some of us feel trapped by our work because of the constraints of working during the week. But why? What happened to working when we feel most inspired? What happened to work being an extension of who we truly are? What happened to our work being a passion project, a life dream, a life purpose? Most of us, at least in North America, leave our personal time to once a year, known as the "vacation." For many, a vacation is an escape from the workplace or from life's challenges rather than an additional experience to the plethora of amazing experiences they have in the pursuit of their passions every day.

Materialism

I think another reason our work looks the way it does, beyond our perspective on busyness, is our obsession with the material world. Materialism has caused many people to be in debt, which keeps us in the energy of needing to make more money or in servitude of someone or something.

Now, it would be easy for me to blame the credit card companies, but we all are at fault. When I was a student, credit was readily available. I knew students who were offered credit limits of $10,000 to $30,000 with nothing to back it up financially. Because I didn't understand the concept behind credit cards, I'm incredibly grateful to my parents, who warned me about the dangers of being in debt. Still, if I'm honest with myself, I see that any debt I created for myself was due to (1) my impatience in wanting my good right now but not believing I could align with it fast enough and (2) the comparison game humans play with one another.

We seem to buy things to demonstrate our worth and fill our emotional voids. The problem with the comparison game is that we never arrive. We constantly must buy more things to one-up whomever we're comparing ourselves with. To keep buying, we have to keep working, which keeps us on the hamster wheel of producing.

The comparison game wasn't as relevant for me as the impatience one. Interestingly, patience is necessary to manifest or align to your dreams. I realize now that impatience is doubt. But back then, I didn't know this. Plus, enjoying the journey was something I struggled with. I wanted my good to happen right now, and of course, because of this, it took longer to arrive than needed. When I tried manifesting strategies, I'd immediately look for the appearance of my desires and got frustrated and upset when they didn't appear. I didn't realize my looking for an external out-picturing was evidence that I didn't believe it was there. You don't look for what you already are.

Another issue with materialism is that we put too much emphasis and focus on what's external. This reinforces the belief that our outside reality is more important than what's happening within us. If we're accumulating, we're happy; otherwise, our joy is stripped from us.

None of this means we shouldn't desire things. It's fun to acquire them; the issue is when those things determine how we feel about ourselves and about our lives. I haven't a clue who said seeing is believing, but they did us a huge disservice. Seeing isn't believing; seeing only keeps us stuck in the reality we may not want to create. When I think of the most extraordinary people I know and of famous historical figures, they all had the gift of believing before they saw. The dreamers, the people who others felt were ahead of their time, who believed in their visions despite contradicting evidence. Our focus on our material world and on immediate gratification keeps us from holding onto our vision, from doing the work of showing up for ourselves when challenges arise on our journey, and from truly tapping into the inner wisdom, knowledge, and treasures that lie within us.

Predictability and safety

My journey through my parents' and my extended family's unpredictable aging process has made me increasingly aware of how comfortable we are with predictability. Although some say they're bored with their lives and want to pursue bigger dreams, we all fear uncertainty to some extent. For example, some would rather stay in employment they hate, fearing they'll not get as many perks in a newer, more aligned workplace.

I believe these fears have to do with our need for safety. We fear others; we fear our world and even ourselves. Our workplaces look the way they do because of our need for security. We need reassurance that every month we'll have money coming in. This was one of the struggles I had in my new business. I didn't know where the money was going to come from, and frankly, that scared me. We don't trust ourselves and the Universe to provide for us, so we sacrifice our freedom, joy, and creativity for the golden handcuffs of good pay and a regular vacation.

I was having a conversation with someone about how miserable they were at work. "Why don't you just leave?" I asked them. This person was a wonderful employee; surely, they could get another job elsewhere.

"Where am I going to get a job with five weeks' vacation?" they replied.

I didn't answer, but what came to my mind was that while they had five weeks of enjoyment, the remaining forty-seven weeks of their year, they were in misery.

As a society, we have come to expect and to welcome predictability, so we work predictable hours and times. We even know, more or less, what the weather will be. By disrupting our routines, the COVID-19 pandemic reminded us how much this habit of doing the same things over and over was keeping us stuck in the same reality and preventing us from truly living our dreams. For us to live our biggest and boldest visions, we must be willing to go into the unknown.

♥ *Heart Stretch*: *Close your eyes, and relax your entire body, beginning from the bottom of your feet all the way to the top of your head. Breathe in and out three times to keep your attention on your body. Now focus on your heart and rest your hand there. From this place, reflect on the following:*

We are often trapped by our own limited thinking, so this exercise will help you become aware of your perceived limits. Now think of the boldest, most outlandish dream you could have. Use the following questions as a guide.

- *What if you could find a job that not only gives you five weeks' vacation but also enriches your soul?*
- *What if you could make more money than you are making currently?*
- *What if you could start an amazing business and never worry about money?*
- *What if you never worried about the things you worry about now?*

As you start to think bolder and bolder, your rational mind may give you all the reasons your dream won't work. Don't worry about those fears. Write them down as well as your dream. We will revisit this dream in later chapters.

I started this chapter with a quote from the Buddha about our main beliefs, feelings, and imaginings. Clearly, our main collective beliefs are limiting beliefs about our work and lives; our main feelings are fear of the unknown and of lack; and our main imaginings focus on the material world, our busyness, and our impatience with life. Our work reflects who we are at every moment, even though we're not aware of it. The way we currently work also reflects just how much we have separated what we do from our true selves.

To reimagine how we work, we have to be willing to look at ourselves and understand how these thoughts, feelings, and imaginings have contributed to the way things are in our lives. We must be willing to face those difficult emotions and beliefs that have allowed us to allow environments filled with power over approaches, control, and fear. But where to start?

Chapter 3

How Our Consciousness Shapes Our Experiences at Work

One must learn to be discerning with one's own thoughts. We must be able to decipher truth versus the lies in our minds. Otherwise, we become enslaved to the shackles of struggles we place on our own ankles.
~ *Brittainy C. Cherry*

Have you ever attended a meeting with someone, and afterward, it seemed like you both were at different events? What each of you aligned with or placed your attention and energy on during the meeting was different, so you did have two different experiences under the same circumstances. I wonder if this explains why children living in the same household can grow up with vastly different experiences of their childhoods.

Our perceptions are caused by our beliefs and thoughts. These thoughts and beliefs create our reality in two ways. First, they align our energy to attract things that coincide with the same thoughts and beliefs (the law of attraction); second, the mind filters out any experiences that contradict those thoughts and beliefs because the mind doesn't like to be wrong (confirmation bias). Thus, what we consider "reality" is really a filtered view of one possible reality. The majority of us, though, are unaware we're aligning to our reality every day. That's because we're creating unintentionally rather than being conscious creators in our lives.

For example, our need for security and our fear of not having enough education may unintentionally lead us to attract employment where we're undervalued or not treated with respect. Or we may create a business where we're constantly grinding it out to attract more clients because we're worried about not having enough. This isn't consciously chosen, as nobody would choose to be underpaid or underappreciated or work themselves to the point of exhaustion.

In fact, most of our experiences have been manifested subconsciously. To understand how our level of conscious awareness has led us to create workplace environments that are not in alignment with who we are, we have to understand what consciousness is. But first, I want to share how I came to this realization through the most bizarre experience.

What is real?

My husband, David, and his sister, Lisa, had signed up to attend classes on metaphysics and spirituality. I'd always felt a close connection to God/Source/Universe but was afraid of anything "spiritual," thinking it was akin to the dark arts. When I was younger, someone in my life was into practices I considered strange or frightening—for instance, praying to a skull in a little house the person kept at home. As an adult, I wasn't open to anything that wasn't provable. In fact, the reason I completed a research degree was that I staunchly believed in evidence.

So, I accompanied my husband to some of the classes, mostly out of curiosity, with no clear intention of participating or believing it would have any impact on me.

During a meditation exercise, we were asked to close our eyes and astral travel (travel with our minds) to wherever we wanted to go. Before I knew it, I was in a dark space—a void, if I may—where I felt a level of peace I'd never experienced before. I wasn't thinking at all, though I was resting. I'd left everything behind and was in complete and total calm. I wasn't my body, or my identity, or anything. I was just consciousness, taking a holiday from everything in my life.

Suddenly, I heard a voice. "It's time to come back," the voice said to me.

"No, I'm good here," I responded mentally. Since I suffered from terrible anxiety, I welcomed the mental break—and I wasn't giving it up.

"You have to come back. You have children, and they need you," the voice said.

"Hmmm." I had to think about this one. Part of me didn't want to leave the incredible peace I was feeling. I couldn't bear to feel the heaviness of worry and fear once again. But my love for my children was a strong pull. Long ago, I decided I'd do anything in my power to ensure I was there for them. So, I came back from wherever I was.

When I opened my eyes, the whole class was staring at me. "You didn't want to come back," said our teacher, Jean. I was surprised, as I wasn't fully convinced this had not been my imagination.

When David and I got home, our babysitter was distraught.

"Your daughter had a hard time sleeping," she said. "She just kept repeating, 'Mommy isn't coming back.'"

This event helped me realize that we're so much more than what we're made to believe. I'm not my body, or this identity, or anything I have attached to. The experience also helped me understand how separated we are from our true selves at work: on Monday morning, I got dressed and went back to work, business as usual, although I'd been profoundly impacted by what happened that weekend.

♥ *Heart Stretch*: *Close your eyes, and relax your entire body, beginning from the bottom of your feet all the way to the top of your head. Breathe in and out three times to keep your attention on your body. Now focus on your heart and rest your hand there. From this place, answer the following:*

- *Have you ever experienced something that you couldn't explain? Or that didn't fit with your current definition of reality?*
- *Did you dismiss it or hide it from others?*
- *Did it alter how you viewed other aspects of your life?*
- *If you didn't have a spiritual or hard-to-explain event, would you be open to experiencing the unexpected?*

Consciousness and reality

My experience with the void taught me that we are consciousness that has a mind and a body. Our consciousness has a relationship to our body in that our thoughts direct our energy and align it to what happens in the physical world. In his book *Psycho-Cybernetics,* Maxwell Maltz discusses the power of visualization in helping us achieve physical outcomes.[1] He describes a research experiment where two groups of people used two different approaches to improve their basketball free throws. The first group practiced physically throwing the ball into the hoop every day. The second group only mentally practiced the free throw. After twenty days, the mental only group improved almost as much as the physical only group did. This isn't surprising, as many elite athletes use the power of mental training and visualization to achieve success. The study, however, reflects something much deeper: the connection between thoughts and physical matter. Thinking without accompanying physical activity caused the body to perform 23 per cent better than not thinking about making successful throws.

I'm grateful, however, that every thought doesn't immediately turn into reality—otherwise, our lives would be way more chaotic than we already make them. However, thoughts that we continue to think over and over, and that have a lot of emotion attached to them, align us to a specific vibration or wavelength which aligns us to a specific reality. What makes some thoughts manifest (turn into reality) over others is the level of attention and energy we have attached to the thought. Negative emotions magnetize negative events and demagnetize positive events because we give them a lot of energy. Said another way, emotions with a lot of gravity tend to pull to them the desires that align with those emotions. For example, the more we worry about something, the more we attract it.

Reimagining how we work begins with us and our consciousness because the world we experience is based on our perceptions of reality. The good news, though, is that we're never stuck. Our current reality is but one of endless possibilities that exist in each current moment.

How we (subconsciously) create our reality at work

I was struggling with a particular group of workers at an organization where I was employed. This group seemed to express resistance to new ideas and often seemed adversarial when leadership made suggestions. Seeking to understand the behavior, I chatted with someone with greater knowledge of these individuals. This person explained that many years ago, a leader had treated this group very poorly. This group was obviously hurt by the treatment and didn't feel valued. However, what the group didn't realize was that they were keeping this story alive and the conflict within it years later through their thoughts and beliefs about their own self-worth. Even though that leader was no longer with the organization, the group had integrated their belief of not being valued into their identity. They believed that anything management did confirmed the old story that they were not valued. Actions that demonstrated otherwise were dismissed as over-compensation. This group had identified so thoroughly with the incident that they couldn't see beyond their perspectives as victims. They couldn't see just how much they had been appreciated, loved, and valued at the organization since their original experience.

The worst part was that their behavior had created and then perpetuated a new story in management: that this group was resistant and insubordinate. When management responded from this perspective, it confirmed the group's perspective that they were not valued. This ended up being a self-fulfilling prophecy.

Every day at work, our thoughts and beliefs shape our identities and determine what we attract to ourselves. This works similarly to the way a radio performs. A radio has an antenna and dials that pick up specific stations. All the radio stations are actually playing all the time, everywhere. However, listening to all of them at once would be overwhelming, so we tune the dial to the specific station that we want to hear. In the example above, this group of workers had set their radio stations to "everyone believes we're expendable." Because they were stuck on that station, they didn't hear anything that didn't align with what was played on that frequency. I had a similar but positive experience while writing this book. I was so in tune with what I was writing that ideas would come to me, often at night while asleep and during my meditation.

How many times have our own fear-based thoughts and negative emotions led to self-fulfilling prophecies? The stories we tell ourselves about who other people are and who we are shape how we interact with others and how we view the world. Our beliefs and the emotions they create energetically align us to environments that reinforce what we believe. While this can make us feel bad, especially when we fully understand our role in creating the problems in our lives, it also reminds us we have the power to change it at any moment. By changing our vibration and focusing our energy on what we want to create, we can better align with our dreams.

> ❤ *Heart Stretch*: *Close your eyes, and relax your entire body, beginning from the bottom of your feet all the way to the top of your head. Breathe in and out three times to keep your attention on your body. Now focus on your heart and rest your hand there. From this place, reflect on your predominant thoughts and feelings. Monitor for at least half an hour.*
>
> - *Write out your most common thoughts and feelings.*
> - *Do you wake up with these thoughts?*
> - *Do you go to sleep with these thoughts?*
> - *Now extend this exercise to your work. What are your most dominant thoughts at work?*

Chapter 4

Living in the Flow

Those who flow as life flows know
they need no other force.
~ Lao Tzu

Over the years, I've noticed that those who believe in "hard work" have a hard time letting go of this identity, even after they become successful. When things are easy for them, they become stressed because this goes against their attachment to the idea that the grind is the only way to achieve. Although their goal was to make enough money to be set for life, ironically, they often don't allow themselves to enjoy the fruits of their labor. Underneath this may be the fear that letting up means they may lose all their achievements.

On the other hand, in my twenty-year journey through the workplace, I've also observed people who were truly living their dreams. These people seemed few and far between. The lucky ones. Now I realize that this opportunity is available to every single one of us.

Living and working from the flow

I've always had two approaches to life. The first one was constantly hustling and looking for opportunities to advance in my workplace. At work and in my personal life, I believed that I had to make things happen for myself and that nobody was going to help me get there. Like my parents, I subscribed to the belief that I had to work harder than anyone I knew. But sometimes this approach didn't work. I'd push harder due to my belief in the struggle, but eventually, I'd get tired of seeing no results. I was out of ideas.

At that point, I'd use my second approach: I'd turn to God/Source/Universe. Asking the Universe/Source/God for my desire and releasing my request was a last-minute attempt at getting what I wanted when I had no idea what to do. Sometimes not knowing is a wonderful gift. It opens us up to potentials we may not have thought of. When I think back on those experiences, I can see that I aligned to many incredible things in this way, with little effort on my part. From aligning to my perfect partner after writing a list of attributes to finding my special type of dog (Doberman Shepherd), to getting large sums of money from unexpected places and circumstances to finding my path when I was lost in another country. I've used my ability to align to my good when I needed it the most. My manifestations came to fruition when I believed it was done and let it go. This has led me to wonder whether the idea of allowing, instead of grinding it out, is more in alignment with who we are and how we desire to create. Maybe we're not meant to work? Or at least not work as hard?

Manifesting my "dream" job

One of my favorite manifestation stories is how I found what was then my dream job. Since age fifteen, I'd dreamed of making a difference in the child welfare field and had specific ways in which I hoped to realize this goal. I didn't want to do direct client work, and I didn't want to get a social work degree.

After working in the same research job for six years, I was facing layoffs. I'd brought money into the organization, which meant they were able to keep me on for an additional year thanks to those funds. By then, I'd given up on my dream of working in the child welfare field, assuming that only people with social work degrees (which I would not end up completing until much later) would be eligible. I applied to any position I could get my hands on, and for an entire year, I kept coming up second. Looking back, if any of those organizations had hired me, I would not have ended up getting my dream job. I'm forever grateful for the beautiful way that life works out for us, but at the time, I wasn't so grateful. My partner and I had two young children under five; we had mouths to feed and bills to pay. We needed both incomes to survive.

Finally, after a year of attending job interviews and not getting hired, I was burned out. I remember yet again feeling like I had no other option than to go inward. I told myself, "I will take two months off from interviews, have an amazing Christmas, and start over in the New Year."

The minute I made the decision to let go, to relax, everything changed. The following week, I saw a post for a job at a Child Welfare

Agency requesting a Quality Assurance Manager. The job description included everything I'd been doing in my previous research jobs and what I'd learned in school. This job was also in the same salary range I desired, which was $20,000 more than I was already making. I attended the job interview and had a great time. On my drive home, I realized I'd dreamed about the job interview the night before. In the dream, I had been interviewed by four smiling people, one of whom had white hair. That was exactly what had occurred during my job interview in reality. At that point, I knew that I had the job before they even called me. Interestingly, I later learned that during the year I was interviewing at other organizations, they were putting the ad together to attract the perfect person for this new position within their organization. If I'd let go and trusted, I'd have had an easier experience.

♥ *Heart Stretch*: *Close your eyes, and relax your entire body, beginning from the bottom of your feet all the way to the top of your head. Breathe in and out three times to keep your attention on your body. Now focus on your heart and rest your hand there. From this place, answer these questions:*

- *What if all our manifestations could be easy? What if we could just set an intention and allowed the Universe to help us attract it?*
- *Have you ever received an unexpected gift? Did something come to you with little or no effort on your part? Remember that not all manifestations are large, some are small but meaningful.*

Tapping into our passions

Many people have tapped into their passions. They are living their dreams and accomplishing this from flow rather than grinding it out. You can tell those who are living their dreams because of the joy and pleasure they exude when they speak about their workplace or careers. They love the journey, not just the destination. This is beyond loving what you are doing. This is loving each step on the path to getting you to where you want to be. If everyone realized the Universe fully supported them to live their dreams and felt they were worthy of having their dreams come true, the world would be different.

Now, when you speak to people who have successfully manifested their dream life, some will say, "Hey, I work hard," which is most likely true. Working hard is a choice. You can work hard or not work hard. But while working hard is exhausting, creating from the flow isn't draining at all, even if you work twelve hours a day. This is because working on what brings us joy invigorates us. Our inner understanding knows there are better ways to attract our dream lives than grinding it out at a job we dislike. This is why many people have gravitated toward manifestation tools and techniques like *The Secret* and *The Universe Has Your Back*.[1]

Have you ever been single and couldn't find a date to save your life, but once you were with someone, people started appearing, desiring to be with you? It's because your energy changed, and you were no longer looking for what you lacked. You were in the energy of receivership.

Living in the flow means being open to opportunities in a relaxed, expansive, and fun manner. It means understanding that everything is working in our favor, and there are no failures. Everything is either a re-direction or a matter of timing. Many of us have examples of when things we desired magically came to us or life aligned in surprising ways. All my supposed failures were blessings in disguise. Working this way allows us to see opportunity everywhere and begin to trust. Trusting that our dreams are coming true also helps us enjoy the success of others. Being in service, loving others, and making good money are not mutually exclusive.

Redefining wealth

I'm not only challenging my own perspective on work but also changing my concept of wealth and how we acquire it. In the workplace, I often see the perspective that you have to work to earn money. But this belief keeps us capped because we can only "work" so much in a day or in a year. Now more than ever, people, especially the younger generation, are looking for passive income. We are also realizing, as a collective, that aligning with more than one source of income can help us in challenging circumstances (such as a pandemic). People are looking to work smarter and not harder. Staying in the energy of wealth helps us to maintain a steady flow of income. For the truly wealthy people I know, their wealth comes from everyone and everywhere in a number of different ways.

Though money is important, and we're grateful to have it, David and I were chatting recently about what abundance means. To us, true wealth means freedom. Most people don't want to be wealthier; they want to be free. True wealth means the freedom to do what I want, when I want it, and with whom I want to do it. The freedom to share with others and to truly live my dreams. True freedom comes with extraordinary relief that everything is taken care of. But how many of us are truly free? We certainly don't work in a way that's freeing. We also often mistake abundance with lots of money, and yes, they can go together, but not always. How many people are rich but are trapped by their money, not free to do whatever they want? Rather, they're caught in the need to make more and more money.

> ♥ *Heart Stretch*: *Close your eyes, and relax your entire body, beginning from the bottom of your feet all the way to the top of your head. Breathe in and out three times to keep your attention on your body. Now focus on your heart and rest your hand there. From this place, answer these questions:*
>
> - *What stories did your parents tell you about money? What stories did they tell you about what abundance means?*
> - *We give so much power to money to help us get the things we desire. Have you ever received something for free or via barter (legally, of course!)?*
> - *How do you define abundance? Describe all the ways you are already wealthy.*
> - *What would it feel like to never worry about money? Stay in that feeling.*

Energy is the new currency

What do I mean when I say energy is the new currency? We believe money is primarily the way we attain things. But what if I told you, that's not the primary way. I'm talking about the way attention helps us create our reality. If our attention directs our energy and thoughts, what we choose to focus on and think about then becomes the radio station we set our dial to. What this means is that what we place our attention on matters greatly. Our emotions then give those thoughts energy, and the energy attracts the event or "station" to us.

So, if energy is what gives our dreams life and enables them to flourish, then how much time am I investing my currency into what I want to create? Unfortunately, we often focus on what we don't want rather than on our desires. At one point, I noticed that I misspent a lot of my energy on worry, fear, doubt, as well as on social media, the news, and other distractions. This was instead of focusing on what I did want to happen.

Human beings tend to obsess about the things they fear. However, this approach is counterintuitive. I believe this is why most anti-anything programs don't work. The wars on crime, drugs, and addiction have not worked because our attention, hence our energy, has been on resisting the old rather than creating the new. We are feeding what we dislike instead of placing our attention or currency on what we want to flourish, things like love, compassion, unity, and equality.

> ♥ **Heart Stretch**: *Close your eyes, and relax your entire body, beginning from the bottom of your feet all the way to the top of your head. Breathe in and out three times to keep your attention on your body. Now focus on your heart and rest your hand there. From this place, do this exercise: For half an hour, watch where you put your attention. Ideally, do this all day or for as long as possible.*
>
> - *What percent of your time and attention did you place on social media?*
> - *What percent of your time and attention did you place on things or people you dislike?*
> - *What percent of your time and attention did you place on things you love or like?*
> - *What percent of your time and attention did you place on your dreams?*
>
> *Do these percentages represent where you desire to spend your energy?*

Aligning with our abundance

Some of us have been playing with the concept of aligning with our abundance—for example, money and other desires coming to us from everyone and everywhere. It means that money can come from unexpected places without you working for it. I started to contemplate this possibility after a surprising event occurred during a declutter challenge.

The Universe doesn't like a vacuum?

Have you heard this saying: "The Universe doesn't like a vacuum and will rush in to fill an empty space?" I never understood it until I tried a twenty-eight-day declutter challenge. The challenge was to donate/trash twenty-one things, every day, for twenty-eight days. By the twenty-eighth day, I was proud of myself and felt quite happy about having discarded so many items I wasn't using. I also realized how I tended to hoard "good things" to use in the future, and decided to use up everything I was saving. I already felt gifted by the experience, so imagine my surprise when people started giving me items to replace what I had let go of. I received three practically new pairs of shoes from someone who had never used them. I'd also gotten rid of many books in my library and had empty spots on the shelf. I'm an avid reader and was certain I'd have to purchase books to fill those spots eventually, but it turned out I didn't need to. At a retreat I attended, they were giving away tons of brand-new books on meditation, spirituality, and mindfulness written by the monks who were leading the retreats. I think I returned with more books that I'd gotten rid of.

Now, when I mention getting something for nothing, I often get resistance: "What do you mean you are not working for it?" or "What if I hurt someone by aligning to a particular manifestation when I get large sums of money." Even if they use the affirmation "for the good of all concerned," some people may still not be comfortable with the idea. I love chatting about this because it reveals to me where people are in their journey toward tapping into their true abundance.

Getting something for nothing can be hard to accept if you are used to "earning" your income. You may feel guilty receiving unexpected money without working at it. You may feel uncomfortable with this discussion since working for our money is so ingrained in our culture. My advice: Allow yourself to experience these feelings without resistance.

We often see getting money for nothing negatively except for winning the lottery. People who receive disability payments or welfare are often regarded as if they're taking advantage of the system because it costs the taxpayers money. In our minds, the money has to come from somewhere in the physical. The intent of social assistance, however, is to be of support as people work toward living their dreams or improving their life circumstances, especially after a loss. Research on basic income has illustrated that people use the money primarily to return to school or to move forward with their dreams rather than to stay on assistance. Often these programs are not expanded nationally due to unfounded fears[2]. However, the programs could be of enormous benefit as individuals transition to better and better positions.

Even though there may be individuals who would rather live on social assistance, nobody who perceives themselves as able to live their dreams and who desires increasing abundance wants to stop at social assistance as it limits our growth and expansion. When we release the fear of not having enough, we can open ourselves to the potential abundance that exist everywhere. I share this to plant seeds of the possibility of the money being there when you need it.

Another reason for our difficulty accepting money for nothing is our sometimes-negative relationship with money. In his pivotal book, *Happy Money,* my friend Ken Honda talks about how people's relationship with money impacts their ability to receive their abundance.[3] When I was a child, my parents had an interesting relationship with money: they desired it but thought it was hard to come by. I viewed having a lot of money as something bad. Why? Because my examples of truly wealthy people were those who had come to this wealth off the backs of others. So, I made good money because I felt I earned it with my high education; however, my willingness to bring in money was capped because I thought having too much money would attract negative life experiences. I now see these limiting beliefs as untrue. I know many people who have aligned with their abundance by serving others and continue to live by values of dignity, respect, love, and compassion for all.

I once heard Ken Honda say that his mentor, Wei Takeda, Japan's Warren Buffet, believed that money takes on different stages. It can be like ice; we feel like we have to grind it out, chip away at it. Most of the world's population lives here. As our relationship with money improves, wealth flows like streams of water into our lives. How well it flows depends largely on whether we place barriers to the flow through our fears and belief in lack. Lastly, once we have a better relationship with money, it's like air: it's everywhere, and it comes from everyone.

Recently, I learned that this concept is similar to the ice/water/steam exercise taught in Qigong for physical well-being. Ice is often related to tension in our bodies. As the energy frees up, it becomes water, and our life force begins to flow. Then the water turns to steam, purifying the energy. The steam is about the alchemy of transformation. I believe there's a direct energy between where we are physically and how much abundance we allow ourselves to flow to us. In my experience, as I began addressing trapped emotions in my body, I started seeing all other areas in my life begin to flow. Allowing money to come to us easily is the path, I believe, we were all meant to take. We are meant to live our dreams and follow our greatest excitement. In order to do so, however, we can't be held back by our fears.

♥ *Heart Stretch*: *Close your eyes, and relax your entire body, beginning from the bottom of your feet all the way to the top of your head. Breathe in and out three times to keep your attention on your body. Now focus on your heart and rest your hand there. From this place, answer these questions:*

- *How do you feel about receiving money for nothing?*
- *Imagine you were to receive $10,000 from a friend or from someone who appreciates your work. How would you feel?*
- *What if someone you didn't know but who knew you left you a big inheritance? Would you accept it?*

Allow yourself to feel any discomfort that arises. Don't judge it. Merely observe. Write it down if that helps you.

Money and self-love

Along my journey toward understanding my relationship with money, I've also realized its connection to self-love. Many of us don't allow ourselves to flourish because of issues of worthiness. Originally, I didn't understand why I wasn't living from my flow consistently. Then one day, I received an unexpected answer. During meditation, I heard myself say: "I am not worthy to live all my dreams." Of course, I now know this isn't true, but it was good to observe what I was subconsciously believing; these beliefs explained why I wasn't allowing the manifestation of my dreams with ease and grace. I felt I had to fight for everything I received.

Many people I've worked with and spoken to feel this way too. I wonder if earning our living is tied to the belief that we must earn the love of others. If we as children learned we needed to behave to earn our parents' love, affection, and attention, then we may not have felt worthy of receiving without action on our part. But the sun shines upon everyone, big or small. Nature offers us whatever we need for free. Or as Louise Hay used to say, "We do not earn the right to breathe, it's just there for us"—ready for when we need it. We are inherently worthy, but we don't always feel this way. And when we go out into the world of work, we bring these beliefs with us.

I've met many people who truly believe they're not enough. Sometimes rather than deal with their difficult emotions of their feelings of worthiness, they justify their lack of achievement as due to external factors (bad economy, low interest in their work). Beliefs about our unworthiness may bring up challenging emotions, such as shame and guilt, and may feel too big to manage. Thus, we focus instead on justifying our perceived limitations. If we have ever said to ourselves, "I'd like to do X, but I don't have enough education, experience, knowledge, money and so on to do Y," then we're limiting ourselves with our beliefs. The problem with these limiting beliefs is that they may hide a more dangerous belief in a lack of worthiness to live your dreams. Why do I believe this? I've observed and learned about countless individuals who have done a lot more with a lot less. Many successful entrepreneurs didn't graduate high school, and people with no funds were able to find ways to get their dreams funded. Due to some H.R. shortages, some organizations may be more interested in your willingness to learn, adaptability, flexibility, ingenuity, or passion than in your work experience or education. Right now, more than ever, the world is ripe with opportunities if we're willing to examine our subconscious thoughts, difficult emotions and give ourselves a real chance on our dreams.

> ♥ *Heart Stretch*: *The following practice is a variation on the self-compassion break suggested by Chris Germer and Kristen Neff in* Teaching the Mindful Self-Compassion Program (2019).[4] *Do this meditation to address difficult emotions as you answer the remaining questions in the book.*
>
> *Close your eyes, and relax your entire body, beginning from the bottom of your feet all the way to the top of your head. Breathe in and out three times to keep your attention on your body. Place your hand on your heart. Ask yourself, directing*

your focus to your heart: "What am I feeling right now?" or "What is going on for me?" Once you answer, offer yourself some reassuring words such as "This is hard" or "This hurts." Then ask your heart, "What do I need in this moment?"

Note: It's important to ask your heart, not your mind, because your mind will project it out. For example, if you are feeling sad, the mind may say, "I need Joe to stop being such a jerk," instead of "I need reassurance because I feel sad." Once the heart tells you what it needs, give it to yourself in an affirmation: either in the form "May I be happy, or may I feel safe" or in the form "I am happy, I am safe."

From this place of inquiry, reflect on:

- *What role does self-love play in allowing you to receive abundantly?*
- *What stories may you be telling yourself about your own worthiness of living your dreams?*

Sometimes, it can be challenging to listen to our hearts. If it feels uncomfortable, just allow yourself to breathe through those feelings. Lean into those challenging feelings. If it feels too big, stop and try again another day.

Chapter 5

Discovering Compassion

Until you have real compassion,
you cannot recognize love.
~ Bob Thurman

My sister and I were watching a conversation between two people we cared deeply about. I was 15 at the time and upset about the conflict. I pulled my sister aside to complain, and she lovingly said to me: "You know, Gissele, your relationship with each of them is your relationship with them. And their relationship to one another is theirs. Their arguments do not need to impact you. You can still have a good relationship with both of them."

I'd just received my first lesson on compassion and didn't know it.

Defining compassion

Everyone is on their own journey. We have no idea of the true purpose of another person's life, so often our assistance comes with provisos. Sometimes the most loving thing one can do is let people fall and live their life no matter what that looks like for them, knowing that it may be exactly what they chose and what they need to experience to step up into their true power. However, we can find it difficult to watch people suffer. This is where the difference between empathy and compassion comes in.

My and David's concept of compassion differs from most. According to the research, compassion is being aware of suffering and desiring to alleviate that suffering through action.[1] For me, this definition is too focused on the suffering aspect of our journeys. I've also seen people misuse this definition to impose their will on others or influence how they act or behave. Often, we give people what we think they need or what we would wish for them instead of what they say they need.

Empathy and compassion, from my perspective, are not the same, though the terms are often used interchangeably. To illustrate the difference more clearly between compassion and empathy, consider the following analogy. Suppose you are rowing your boat on a calm lake when suddenly, you observe someone drowning. Empathy is akin to you jumping in the lake with the drowning person to help save them. Feeling empathy activates brain receptors that mirror the pain you perceive in another person.[2] Compassion, on the other hand, is akin to you staying in the boat and helping the drowning person get on board your boat. The person may choose not to get on the boat, but that's their choice. Compassion enables us to see the best version of the other person possible, whether they choose to accept our vision of them or not.

When I was younger, I used to derive my own personal value from helping and believed that I had to suffer with those I observed suffering. This eventually became unbearable to me since there's so much suffering in the world. I also realized I wasn't helping anyone with my own suffering. I was only contributing more suffering to the issue. Additionally, when we give to others but we don't want to or feel like we can't, this can lead to burnout.[3] Expecting to help too many people only leads to us drowning too. A change in perspective, however, has helped me stay on the boat and be of greater assistance than drowning with people suffering ever could. The gift of nonjudgment or acceptance also allowed me to see beyond the known and open myself to other perspectives about suffering.

A word about compassion fatigue. Sometimes, although we may believe we're acting out of compassion (staying on the boat), we are, in fact, jumping in the lake (experiencing empathy) and drowning ourselves as we try to help the other person. On the other hand, it's possible to have too many drowning people in the lake and not enough boats. Not having enough boats can create what some call compassion fatigue. Allowing ourselves to stay with these uncomfortable feelings and reaching out to others to provide assistance to those who are drowning is a great way of not falling into the trap of jumping into the water.

♥ *Heart Stretch*: *Close your eyes, and relax your entire body, beginning from the bottom of your feet all the way to the top of your head. Breathe in and out three times to keep your attention on your body. Now focus on your heart and rest your hand there. From this place, reflect on compassion:*

- *What does compassion mean to you?*
- *What is the most compassionate thing you have ever done for someone?*
- *What is the most compassionate thing someone has done for you?*
- *What aspects of compassion feel challenging?*

The myth of tough love

"Everybody gets a ribbon!" my husband said to me, clapping his hands laughing as we chatted about our kids' extracurricular activities. He was teasing me for my desire to eliminate competition in sports. David grew up in a pull-yourself-up-by-your-bootstraps type of household. It took a long time for him to get in touch with his more compassionate side and realize he didn't have to motivate himself or the children with criticism or harshness, even though he still appreciates the fun of competition. For a long time, we both believed that tough love and criticism were the best ways to motivate ourselves to perform well and flourish. We bought into the belief that our parents' pushing or lack of it had led us to where we were.

As a collective society, we have told ourselves many lies about the power of "tough love" and criticism. We believe that criticism allows us to achieve our best. Not surprisingly, workplace cultures frequently celebrate both the grind and toxic behavior. For example, I once heard a famous chef talk about how their mentors would throw food at them and how nowadays the younger generation were "snowflakes" for not accepting this behavior. They are called snowflakes because they melt under pressure. Some individuals have attributed their career success to the fact that they were treated with harshness. I'm here to tell you those individuals succeeded despite the toxic treatment, not because of it. The mark of a truly effective strategy is whether it has worked for the majority of people who used it. Most who experienced the tough-love work environment didn't succeed, and some ended up committing suicide, living with eating disorders, going on sick leave, or failing out of the industry. Others developed negative relationships with clients.

We may believe toxic work environments lead to success simply because the few individuals that survived attribute their success to toughing it out. However, this is a well-known fallacy called post hoc ergo propter hoc, which means "after it therefore because of it." It was perhaps the person's willingness to not allow the toxic behavior to crush them, rather than the toxic behavior per se, that contributed to the individual's success.

There is another way that's more motivating and leads to greater achievement than "tough love" or "power over" approaches. More and more research supports the finding that love and compassion motivate us better than power over approaches do. Why? First, fear narrows our views, so we tend to believe we have limited options during the most challenging moments. Love and compassion, however, enable us to regulate difficult feelings so we can expand our view of a situation. They keep us going during adversity. Many businesses survived COVID-19 because they cared about their staff and made choices for overall well-being.

Additionally, when we motivate ourselves with love, we focus more on the joy of creating than on criticizing ourselves for not performing. Toxic workplace behavior has less to do with attempting to motivate others and more to do with leaders' or mentors' inability to regulate themselves internally when things don't go their way. It can feel like a giant tantrum that some leaders have at work, and people accept this behavior for many reasons: fear, ignorance, and victim consciousness. This isn't an attempt to judge those individuals but rather an illustration of how outward toxic work behavior reflects our inability to address our difficult feelings and thoughts.

> ♥ *Heart Stretch*: *Close your eyes, and relax your entire body, beginning from the bottom of your feet all the way to the top of your head. Breathe in and out three times to keep your attention on your body. Now focus on your heart and rest your hand there. From this place, reflect on tough love and motivation:*
>
> - *How do you motivate yourself to perform your best?*
> - *How do you motivate others to perform their best?*
> - *Do you use criticism, judgment, or love?*
> - *Whose voice do you hear around your performance? Is it yours or someone else's?*

The myth of professionalism

Ah . . . professionalism. Such a loaded word. When I entered the workforce, professionalism was akin to emotional distance. To be professional meant you were always calm and didn't demonstrate any "difficult" emotions. This was mirrored in research work and in the belief that you could truly be unbiased and completely separate yourself from your research. Now we're beginning to understand that we can never truly be objective, as our perceptions and our beliefs influence the outcomes we see.

The separation of our emotional lives from our work has, I believe, led to the dehumanization of the workplace. If I can't see myself as a human being, with all my difficult feelings, and can't validate my emotions in the workplace, I will certainly not be able to do that for another person. To avoid being emotional, I must dehumanize myself and the people around me, seeing them as widgets or nonhumanoid things. I can't be unemotional at work and at the same time be in resonance with or be impacted by someone else's feelings.

We have become so uncomfortable with our own emotions, including at work, that we sometimes use outside tools to suppress them, like drugs and alcohol. But these are not the only ways we suppress our challenging feelings. We may use distractions like social media, emotional eating, overspending, or other strategies that keep us from the present moment. The belief in professionalism has created a wall between ourselves, our colleagues, and our clients. Worse, it has disconnected us from ourselves and our own needs. Some of us no longer trust ourselves at work.

Instead of so-called professionalism, a better approach is equanimity: mental calmness in the face of adversity. Equanimity is emotional fortitude that comes from harmony between our minds and bodies. It means reflecting, then responding with calmness, giving a person the benefit of the doubt and understanding that in every moment, we have power.

Note that we can't achieve equanimity when we're in denial of our feelings. In fact, we have to face our challenging feelings and address the needs behind them in order to reach the point where we don't give these feelings so much power over us. This can happen only with the practice of self-compassion and self-kindness, refusing to judge ourselves for having uncomfortable feelings. Rather, we can treat our most challenging emotions as guests bringing incredible gifts of growth and opportunity. Even emotional outbursts and misbehavior at work are opportunities for greater love, compassion, and understanding among colleagues.

> ♥ *Heart Stretch*: *Close your eyes, and relax your entire body, beginning from the bottom of your feet all the way to the top of your head. Breathe in and out three times to keep your attention on your body. Now focus on your heart and rest your hand there. From this place, try this or a variation of the strategy below:*

- *Have tea with your feelings: when challenging emotions show up, I envision in my imagination a large table, and all my emotions are invited to sit down. Each one is allowed to speak, and when I feel my body tensing as one of my emotions is speaking, I breathe into the spot to release the feeling. This has enabled me to soften the emotion and allow it to pass much more quickly. After each of my guests is invited to speak, I move to the soothing part of the exercise. I decide to place my hand on my heart and send love to each of those emotions with tender words. I say things like: "Thank you for showing up for me. I know you are giving me feedback about where I am." or "Thank you, I know this made you afraid." I also envision each emotion as a little baby, which I rock and soothe saying, "out of this circumstance, only good things will come. Everything is all right." These actions allow the emotions to release and shift into ease. Lastly, after the most challenging emotions have released, I do some minor meditations during the day, focused on keeping a state of peace for the remainder of the day.*

The myth of weakness and vulnerability

The other myth of love and compassion is that they make us weak and vulnerable. We are so afraid of being seen as vulnerable and taken advantage of that we'll do anything to protect ourselves from our feelings. We avoid being compassionate and loving toward others—

what if this person takes advantage of me? We do this at the expense of addressing our own needs. Now, pain is part of the human experience, so being loving and compassionate will not prevent us from experiencing pain. What it will do, however, is prevent that pain from turning into trauma. It will help us recover faster because compassion reminds us that even in moments when others are attempting to hurt us, we have power.

Compassion for ourselves requires creating and maintaining loving boundaries. This means that when we love ourselves, we'll stand firm on what we want and don't want. Many of us struggle with saying "no" firmly, perhaps due to our need to belong and be accepted. Sometimes we are afraid to say no to avoid feeling the difficult feelings generated by keeping our boundaries. However, in the long run having firm boundaries helps us feel safer, which in turn allows us to show our true selves. That kind of vulnerability enables greater and deeper connection with others.

In my experience, love is by far the most powerful force on earth. To experience something negative and yet not allow it to change us, destroy us, or make us small or someone we don't want to be is a powerful thing. Being truly compassionate and loving not only requires boundaries but also truth. You can't lie to someone and be loving. You can communicate your truth in loving ways, but if you are deceiving someone, you are not loving them. But sometimes we have a hard time standing in our truth. We may not believe that our truth is valuable, or we may worry that the other person will not validate our belief. We also may not be truthful to ourselves because facing our truths may be too difficult. A great starting point to being truthful to ourselves and others is to be willing. Just be willing to see the truth and to tell yourself the truth, and your heart will find ways to show you in a safe and loving way.

The myth of narcissism

I've also heard concerns that self-compassion and self-love are narcissistic and selfish. This isn't true. The long-standing association between self-love and narcissism is actually based on Greek mythology.[4] Narcissus was a god who died because he fell in love with himself. He fell in love with a reflection. Had Narcissus only known that he was already with the person he loved the most, he would not have died. People who act selfishly or narcissistically need to take energy from others to give to themselves. People who truly love themselves give to themselves what they need and don't need anything from others. The paradox is that when you attend to your own needs and allow yourself to live your dreams, you stop being so self-focused. Because all your needs are met, focusing on yourself is a fait accompli. Usually, that's the time when you become completely other focused. You experience joy from helping other people live their dreams, and focus on being truly of service, not because you need something from the other person but because of our interconnectedness. Sharing our joys and our dreams feels good. From a vibrational perspective, it makes sense to help other people too. A vibration is a state of being or energetic quality in a person. It is much easier to keep our vibration high for example feeling joy, happiness, or peace, if others around us are also in high vibrational alignment. It is harder to maintain a high vibration if the world around us is vibrating at a lower level. More clearly stated, we're more likely to get carried away by the negative feelings of others if the majority of people we're with are feeling negative.

When our hearts are filled with love for ourselves, it seeps out to everyone and everything we encounter. Not needing anything on an emotional level does not mean we don't need people in our lives. The people in our lives are gifts. They are our mirrors and alert us to what we're thinking or believing at any moment. We are also here to assist each other in our manifestation journeys.

♥ *Heart Stretch: Close your eyes, and relax your entire body, beginning from the bottom of your feet all the way to the top of your head. Breathe in and out three times to keep your attention on your body. Now focus on your heart and rest your hand there. From this place, reflect on the following:*

- *Revisit the thoughts you had as you read Chapter 4. Has your perspective on self-love changed? Your perspective on living your dreams?*
- *Did you learn any of the myths about compassion from people in your life?*

Sometimes, it can be challenging or uncomfortable to listen to our hearts. It may help to try the exercise in Chapter 4 (see page 46) before you start.

I also invite you to revisit these questions as you continue through the book.

Chapter 6

Compassion for Myself

Yesterday I was clever, so I wanted to change the world.
Today I am wise, so I am changing myself.
~ Rumi

There was a time when I worked in leadership for an organization facing a potential merger. The atmosphere was tense all of the time. We had financial difficulties and were concerned about our ability to continue providing services to our clients. Additionally, we were all worried about our own welfare. Would I still have a job? What would happen to the staff? This period of instability was draining our resources and impacting staff mental health. I was trying to keep the staff informed of the latest developments, but I had no real answers, and this made me uncomfortable. Now, my team and I had a great relationship. I valued their feedback and thought I was offering them the same level of love and care I had before the looming merger. However, one day, a staff member came up to me and asked, "Are you okay?"

I looked at them confused. "Yeah, why?"

"Well," they shifted their body uncomfortably, "you're not there for us anymore. You don't check in like you used to, and your door is always closed."

"Thank you for being honest with me. I appreciate it. I will do better," I replied.

The person smiled and walked away, but I felt hurt by their statement. I'd thought I was making myself available to everyone. Actually, I felt like I was twisting myself like a pretzel to ensure everything was being managed, and here was someone pointing out that I was neglecting the staff.

I took a deep breath. Since I was already practicing compassion and love for myself, held space for my difficult feelings while I listened to the feedback of this person. When I was able to allow my difficult emotions to be there, I realized that what the other person had said was completely true. I was neglecting the team and their well-being. I wasn't able to be there for them because I was barely able to hold it together myself. I'd unconsciously created an atmosphere of unavailability to prevent myself from taking on more than I could emotionally handle. Clearly, I needed time to regroup and put my own oxygen mask on. I needed to take care of myself so that I could be present for the others. I'm forever grateful that this staff member had the courage to tell me so honestly how they felt. They were mirroring back to me what I needed to hear in order to be fully there for others.

Compassion turned inward

"All compassion is self-compassion. Without compassion for yourself, you can't experience compassion for others," my husband, David, would say as we chatted about my work in child welfare. He always dropped gold nuggets for me to digest.

This statement felt true . . . mostly. At times, I struggled with being compassionate to those whom I felt were oppressing me because their behavior seemed so intentional and hurtful. But as I gave to myself the compassion I was seeking, I stopped giving my power away to others, and I realized just how true it is that you can't give to others what you don't have within.

In fact, compassion for others always begins with the self. Why? It would be easy for me to tell you to be compassionate, loving, kind, and generous, but it won't work unless you meet your own needs first. Compassion for the self is compassion turned inward, and it involves being aware of our own hurt and our limiting beliefs, then consciously deciding to support ourselves with kindness, love, and patience and, most importantly, without judgment.

When I first started in child welfare, I thought that if I told some workers to share power and to listen to the voices of families and youth, they could practice in a more loving and compassionate way. However, this didn't make any difference in the interactions between some workers and families. Why was this? This finding made sense once I placed this experience within the context of Maslow's hierarchy of needs. According to Maslow, it's AFTER basic physiological and safety needs are met that the need for love and belonging is strongest[1]. Thus, until a person gets out of survival mode, they can't contemplate being loving and compassionate toward others. Many of the workers in the child welfare field are in survival mode.

But what about all those people who share their food even though they have little? Or people who are the most caring during the most difficult circumstances? Survival mode is a mental state of stress arousal, not an actual physical state. Those individuals may be surviving, but they can't be in survival mode if they're willing to care for others. Even wealthy people can be in survival mode.

This isn't about them. It's about you.

Many of us have heard the saying, "It's not about you; it's about them" in response to an action or interaction that seems undeserved. I've used this to support myself and my loved ones during some difficult times. One of my most challenging discoveries was that this idea is only partly true. When I was growing up, if someone commented about my height, it would never have impacted me because I wasn't worried about my height. However, if anyone said anything that I perceived to be negative about my nose, I would have been hugely triggered. Why? Because I hated my nose and thought something was wrong with it.

Being triggered in that way has been a huge gift to me. It offers me the opportunity to become aware of what I'm choosing to believe and to choose different thoughts and feelings.

Of course, this does not mean people are not responsible for what they say or do. They are. However, we're responsible for how we react to what others say and do to us. This discussion on triggers is about understanding what we're giving power to and why. If anyone comments on my nose now, I don't react at all. Actually, it makes me laugh. I have grown to love my nose. In fact, I love all those aspects of myself that I used to see as my imperfections. They are now my source of greatest strength since I was able to transform what once gave people power over me into what I've chosen to appreciate.

A trigger can be an invitation to realize that something we're thinking or doing is out of alignment with who we really are. It is the gift of awareness that we still have healing to do around what's triggering us. If the issue wasn't about us, we wouldn't be triggered by it at all. We would truly understand that people's reactions or behaviors are about what's going on for them.

*♥ **Heart Stretch**: Close your eyes, and relax your entire body, beginning from the bottom of your feet all the way to the top of your head. Breathe in and out three times to keep your attention on your body. Now focus on your heart and rest your hand there. From this place, reflect on your triggers.*

- *Who or what causes a reaction in you?*
- *What do you think you need when that reaction arises?*
- *What thoughts and beliefs do you have about your triggers?*

Please use the meditation suggested in Chapter 4 if this exercise is challenging.

Practicing self-love and self-compassion

I believe the essence of who we are is loving and compassionate. But we're so far removed from ourselves, we don't recognize that essence anymore. Long ago, we learned about what some call "conditional" love, the belief that we're only loveable if we meet some external need or condition, whether our own or someone else's. We may have picked up these messages from our parents or key people in our lives: for example, you are loveable if you are thin, helpful or compassionate, giving, a good listener, well-behaved, etc. These conditions prevent us from practicing compassion toward ourselves. The truth is this conditional love isn't love at all. It is attachment and expectation. Love has no conditions attached to it.

Once we're able to understand and unconditionally love and accept ourselves through the practice of self-compassion, we can move on to doing the same for others. Unconditionally means that regardless of circumstances or expectations, we're worthy of love and compassion merely because we are. Period. Unconditionally loving others means extending love to other beings without the need that they meet some requirement, including them loving us back.

What does unconditionally loving ourselves look like? For me, it's fully accepting and appreciating myself without the need for me to be different. What does this mean? It means I don't have to change in any way in order for me to accept myself fully. I don't need to be thinner, more compassionate and loving, or more tolerant. I can choose to accept myself just as I am and where I am.

Does this mean we don't want to change? No. We can fully accept ourselves and choose to change something for the fun of it or for the experience of changing. One of the most challenging questions I've asked myself and others is: can we love ourselves even if we don't accomplish anything or contribute anything to the world? Can we look at ourselves with wonder, true appreciation, and joy, or even playfully when we make a mistake? I remember a huge shift in how I treated myself after I made a mistake. Before, I'd beat myself up if I wasn't perfect. However, lately my mistakes, even if they appear stupid, make me laugh out loud at my own goofiness. I'm talking belly laughing to the point where I have to take time to breathe.

Can we see our flaws and our negative behavior with kindness, forgiveness, compassion, and gentleness? Can we talk to ourselves as we would with someone we care deeply about instead of someone who is our enemy? Can we be willing to stop scaring ourselves with our catastrophizing? If we can't, that's okay. We just need to be open to the experience. We need to be willing to love ourselves in whatever way we can. We can no longer afford not to love ourselves and to spill our hurts onto ourselves and other people. The world looks the way it does because of our collective unaddressed trauma.

Our compassion journey is mostly about unlearning all the negative things we have learned and tapping into our truly and unconditionally loving and compassionate selves—who we are at our core. Remember that babies are loving and accepting from the start, then later learn to hate and to fear. Our journey in loving ourselves is about dismantling the barriers that prevent us from being our true selves.

> ♥ *Heart Stretch*: *Close your eyes, and relax your entire body, beginning from the bottom of your feet all the way to the top of your head. Breathe in and out three times to keep your attention on your body. Now focus on your heart, and rest your hand there. From this place, do Louise Hay's mirror exercise[2]. In the morning or in the evening, tell yourself in the mirror how much you love yourself. Tell yourself how wonderful you are and how much you appreciate yourself. In the beginning, this may feel challenging. Keep going, even if you are only able to appreciate yourself a tiny bit. Just be willing to do this for twenty-one days or more.*

I have to admit that I wasn't always aware that I wasn't loving toward myself. Becoming aware of how I was treating myself was the first step in my self-love journey. For many years, I suffered from terrible anxiety and gave all my energy and attention to my fears. I used catastrophic thinking and was always waiting for the other shoe to drop. I didn't trust anybody and didn't believe I could live my dreams. Because I held these beliefs and their accompanying emotions, it's no wonder I had relationship problems. My girlfriend Angie and I were out on our yearly Yorkdale Mall shopping trip many years ago, when we decided to stop for lunch. As we ate our salads, I complained to Ang about my then boyfriend. I was telling her about issues we were having and going on and on about my worries about him leaving me. She listened to me politely and then leaned in. "Why are you doing this to yourself?"

I was taken aback. "What? I'm doing this to myself?"

She smiled and then went back to eating her food.

I hadn't realized my negative thinking was causing me suffering. I was harming myself by living in fear of not being good enough. My experiences with my boyfriend were mirroring back to me what I was thinking and feeling. I had huge fears of abandonment and was the first one to eject from a relationship because I feared getting close to people. However, each time I believed it was my boyfriend's fault. I wasn't aware that even if a negative experience was real to me, the subsequent negative thoughts and endless worrying meant I was re-traumatizing myself.

We worry a lot about physical self-harm, but we may be harming ourselves every day through our negative or scary thoughts. It was only when I started practicing kindness in my way of thinking by not allowing negative thoughts to dictate my life that my life changed.

My journey to self-love has been ongoing. Because the messaging I received growing up was negative, I needed to flip the script on my own catastrophizing and negative viewpoints. I started by reprogramming my brain with positive affirmations. I'd listen over and over to Louise Hay's recordings; her positive, soothing perspective was just what I needed to help me feel at ease when I was afraid. I started the practice of meditation once I realized that soothing myself had to come from within. Otherwise, as long as my soothing came from a source outside of me, I was dependent on it. My husband also used to be a source of soothing for me. I relied on him to reassure me that everything was going to be all right. When he couldn't reassure me or when he wasn't available, I couldn't self-regulate. Over time, I realized I needed to find safety within myself so I didn't require my outside environment to be a specific way.

Meditating helped me find the calm and space between thoughts. An inner calm rose within me when it seemed like storms raged around me. In the beginning, though, meditating felt gritty . . . unpleasant. Over time, just by showing up, it grew easier and more soothing. And I discovered my compassionate and loving voice within me, the one that reminds me of my own inner power and worthiness.

I admit that when an event or interaction that triggered my fears occurred, it was challenging to sit with those uncomfortable emotions and not get sucked in by the fear. After a while, however, I lived more and more boldly and with ease and grace. Positive thinking and loving kindness became like breathing. Things that historically made me afraid no longer affected me. I started to relax and appreciate the moment and the beauty of the fellow human beings who share this earth with me.

❤ Heart Stretch: Close your eyes, and relax your entire body, beginning from the bottom of your feet all the way to the top of your head. Breathe in and out three times to keep your attention on your body. Now focus on your heart and rest your hand there. From this place, reflect on the following:

- *There is no right way to love yourself. Only your heart holds the key to what your journey to self-love will look like. My path has been different from David's and from my children's. To understand your path to self-love, quiet your mind, soothe your body, and allow yourself to open your heart to your inner guidance.*
- *Ask yourself, what can I do to love myself more today? And see what comes up.*

When you begin this journey, it may not feel like you are making any progress. There were times when it seemed I was back where I started, feeling crappy about myself. But when we show up consistently for ourselves every day, something happens on that nth day ... it gets easier, we feel lighter, and then one day, we wake up and say to ourselves, "Wow, I am worthy. I love myself." Showing up for ourselves and our needs takes consistency but has a cumulative effect. Even when we feel like nothing is changing or everything is getting worse, I promise that your life is shifting, positively. We have to commit to staying with those difficult feelings. It is important, though, to titrate your exposure to them. When they get too overwhelming, doing something physical will help you calm the mind and emotions. Even devoting five minutes a day adds up.

Compassion's unexpected impact

When I first began practicing mindful self-compassion, I was doing it to address the suffering I observed at work. As a leader, I wanted to help the staff deal with burnout. What I didn't notice, however, was how much I was suffering both in the workplace and at home. I was unaware that growing up with parents who had experienced various levels of child adversity had impacted me so much that I was harming myself with my focus on fear. It's no wonder I wanted to work within the child-protection system—my inner child was crying out for love and support. Self-compassion helped me give myself what I was looking for externally from others: love, nurture, validation, reassurance, peace. The practice of self-love and self-compassion enabled me to shift my perspective from fear and distrust to a more open, curious, loving, peaceful existence. An unexpected result was that as I shifted, my whole world shifted. My relationships with others became harmonious. I judged people less. I grew more curious about people and opened myself up to love others from my overflow and not from my reserves. I was open and receptive to living my dreams and trusting the flow.

In the example I offered earlier, my colleague didn't judge me for not being present for them and their teammates. They started the conversation with "Are you okay?" They gave me the benefit of the doubt and opened up the dialogue for me to understand how my suffering was impacting my relationship with the staff I was overseeing. For David and me, true compassion is the act of allowing all things to be. It is witnessing all life without judgment with a willingness to understand and support all life and then making the most loving choice possible.

Regret

Regret is a dream killer in many ways. We become so focused on what we didn't accomplish in the past, on an opportunity that we feel we can never get back, that we miss the opportunities available to us at every moment. Beneath regret may be a belief in "not enough." Either there are not enough opportunities (lack), or we're not enough to receive our dreams (worth). Both are untrue. We always have the potential to get back on track to what we truly desire to be.

Of course, we may have to let go of what we think this should look like. For example, if at one point we desired to be a teacher, but we don't want to go back to teacher's college, we can teach others through social media or platforms like Udemy. When we believe things have to be a specific way, we limit ourselves. Barriers like age or education are also solely beliefs. There are always barriers that can be overcome, and who knows, maybe you can be the first! One of the episodes of my podcast, the *Love and Compassion Podcast with Gissele,* featured Greta Pontarelli, ten-time world champion pole dancer who began her career at sixty-seven. If she had listened to people's stories about old age, she would have never taken up pole dancing. She hasn't let age or a bad hip hold her back from achieving her dreams.

I once read in a metaphysics book a discussion on how there's no loss in the Universe. If a door closes for you, there's another one waiting to be opened.[3] This belief always gave me comfort and peace when things didn't work out the way I had envisioned them. And sometimes, not accomplishing what we think we desire may be a blessing in disguise. Sometimes we don't realize that there may be something better out there that's closer to what our heart truly desires. At least this has been true in my life. During the year, I went to job interviews and didn't get hired. All the jobs I interviewed for were great; however, the position I ended up with had everything I wanted: excellent pay and benefits, work that I loved, a great mentor/employer, and so on.

A year ago, I ran a free meditation class on self-compassion, and during one of our sessions, we used a "reimagining" approach to create a desirable outcome from a seemingly negative experience. After the meditation, a student shared her reflection. Debbie paused for a moment and said:

"It was not what I expected."

"What do you mean?" I asked . . . thinking that perhaps the meditation hadn't worked for her.

"Well, the meditation helped me realize that if I had taken the path I regretted not taking, things would not have worked out as I desired, so it was good that I didn't take that path," she said confidently.

This was certainly not what *I* was expecting, but it reminded me that things always work out for the best, even though we don't necessarily see it.

For those struggling with regret, I recommend the following meditation. I also like to use it when I have to make difficult decisions or am unsure where to go next.

> ♥ *Heart Stretch*: *Close your eyes and place your hand on your heart. Now relax your entire body, beginning from the bottom of your feet all the way to the top of your head. Bring to mind the event you regret the most. Now imagine a hallway with multiple doors representing different outcomes, including the door with the outcome that already occurred. Take one of the other doors and allow images to come to your mind. Where does the door take you?*
>
> *When you are ready to release the meditation, you can go back to the hallway and take a different door, or you can choose to go back to your physical self and focus on your body again from the bottom of your feet to the top of your head. When you are ready, open your eyes.*

Chapter 7

Compassion for Others

Compassion is keen awareness of the
interdependence of all things.
~ Thomas Merton

I was away at a cottage when I had a dream about a friend who kept saying, "I need to talk to you." When I woke up and went into the kitchen, I saw I'd received a text from this friend, at that moment, using those exact words.

Have you ever thought of a friend, and they called you later? Or had a predictive dream about someone? This has happened to me more than once. I believe it illustrates that we're all intricately connected in this universal web.

We are interconnected

An economics exam I took in first year university asked us to explain the impact that changing the value of the Canadian dollar would have on the global market. Although I doubt I answered it correctly, the real lesson for me in that question was the understanding of how something that impacts one country and its people can impact all others globally. I've heard Neale Donald Walsh, author of *Conversations with God,* say that "what we do for another, we do for ourselves and what we do for ourselves we do for another."[1] I love this quote because it demonstrates the interconnectedness among all human beings.

My love for my co-workers and desire to alleviate their suffering led me to seek an answer to our workplace issues. I wasn't consciously looking to help myself. I stumbled on compassion, and as I was examining it as a possible solution for my colleagues' woes, I healed myself. When I healed myself, all my relationships healed in turn.

WE ARE INTERCONNECTED

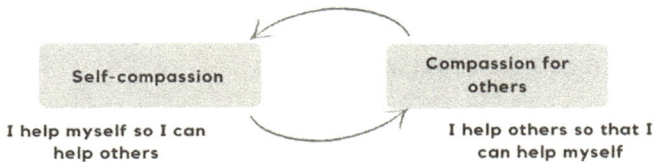

Self-compassion		Compassion for others
I help myself so I can help others		I help others so that I can help myself

The connection between self-compassion and
compassion for others

*Figure 1. The connection between our
own compassion and compassion for others*

My friend Tony McAleer illustrates the interdependence between human beings in his book *The Cure for Hate*.[2] Tony was a key person in establishing many of the systems in Canada that may still exist to spread hate and white supremacy. An act of compassion from a Jewish therapist as well as the love of his children helped him realize that love is more powerful that hate. The unconditional love he experienced led him to abandon white supremacy and work toward spreading greater compassion and unity. When we chatted on the *Love and Compassion Podcast with Gissele*, he told me that when others saw his humanity, it opened the door for him to see it in himself. Tony realized that as long as he was unable to acknowledge his own pain, he couldn't see the pain he caused others. He could do hurtful things to others because he was detached from his own shameful feelings. Once he reconnected with those difficult feelings, he could begin the journey to healing and repairing his relationships with his fellow human beings.

Love and kindness for ourselves are needed to create a world that focuses on addressing the suffering of all human beings, but it works the other way as well. When I help others, I'm helping myself because I too will benefit from a more inclusive world. On the other hand, when I assist myself via self-compassion, I have a greater ability to help others, as my focus will not be on my own fear and survival but rather on our common humanity.

Unfortunately, we're often taught that we're separate from one another and to fear each other. We are taught that life, love, happiness, abundance, and power are all zero-sum games. If others have more, I must automatically have less. This lack mentality has prevented us from living our dreams, and the attention and energy we give to lack has contributed to our belief in competition, scarcity, and failure and kept us stuck in dead-end or toxic workplaces. This belief in not feeling enough has prevented us from loving and having compassion for others.

All of the compassion research I discovered on my quest for a solution to workplace suffering included elements of common humanity. Common humanity refers to the fact that we're all flawed and doing the best we can with what we have. Normally, when we suffer, we feel isolated, as though we're the only ones going through this. The concept of common humanity reminds us that we're never alone.

Common humanity is often discussed among Indigenous peoples:

> "All my relations" is a first reminder of who we are and of our relationship with both our family and our relatives. It also reminds us of the extended relationship we share with all human beings. But the relationships that Indigenous people see go further, the web of kinship extending to the animals, to the birds, to the fish, to the plants, to all the animate and inanimate forms that can be seen or imagined. More than that, "all my relations" is an encouragement for us to accept the responsibilities we have within this universal family by living our lives in a harmonious and moral manner.[3]

I love this quote because it reminds me of our need for balance and harmony with everything. Peace and harmony are missing in the world, but this only reflects the lack of peace and harmony within ourselves. It reflects the chaos in our minds. Creating greater harmony in life, at work, and in the world, begins with calming our minds and not giving so much credence to every thought. It is about learning to work with our emotions to direct our energy toward peace, ease and grace.

Fellowship with all people on earth is the goal of compassion. We have the power to live our dreams and do so in balance with our fellow human beings and the planet. To live this way, however, we must be willing to believe that we can and to address our difficult emotions and negative thinking when they arise.

Eradicating hate may feel like too big of a goal to achieve on our own. But every day, our thoughts and feelings contribute to a world where chaos and strife exist in seemingly small ways. Multiply those negative thoughts and emotions by eight billion people, and we get a world of war, death, and destruction. The key to addressing these issues lies in understanding how we use our energy for separation.

The walls of separation

Many of us feel alone because of the disconnect between ourselves and our fellow human beings. When we see ourselves as "separate," we're more likely to see others as competition, as the other, and as a threat to our very existence. Feeling this way in our businesses or in the workplace will make working with others challenging because beneath these beliefs are fears. Fears of not being enough, not having enough, and not being worthy.

At work, most of the deadly sins are fundamentally unaddressed hurt feelings and uncontrolled fear. For example, envy can be a motivating emotion, but any benefits wear out quickly. Envy can help us identify a desire, but its underlying belief is that others have something we want but can't get. If we believed we could get it, we wouldn't bother with envy at all. The emotion then becomes one of feeling unworthy or not good enough. We could focus our energy and attention on aligning with or going after what we desire instead, but if we feel we don't deserve it, we won't bother shifting out of envy.

When I was younger, I used to envy people who had what I desired. I also would project my envy to others because it was an uncomfortable emotion to face. I felt guilty about it and chose to believe that others were envying me. Once I was honest with myself, I saw that it was the other way around. Being kinder to myself freed me up to see that my envy was caused by a resistance to be where I was. *Why am I not there and they are? What if I never get there? Don't I deserve to be there?* Over time I understood that these were merely beliefs that I need not give power to. I could sit with my discomfort and remind myself of the amazing opportunities that are available at every moment.

Greed is another example of how we separate ourselves from one another. Greed is based on the belief in lack, which was the foundation of many colonization approaches. If colonizers truly believed that they had enough, that their supply was unlimited and always available, they'd never have sought to conquer and take away from others. Those who build their empires by suppressing the wealth of others believe in not having enough to the point where they need to get it from the outside. The irony is, the more money they receive, they more they'll need because they're still in the alignment of not having enough. It is like a hole that can't be filled. And since what we do for others, we do for ourselves, depriving others and trying to keep others down will manifest back to these people in different ways. What do I mean? I mean that because their energy is to take from others, there will be other areas where people will take away from them.

Remember that since energy is currency, spending all our attention on the person we envy or the person who is acting greedy is detracting us from achieving our own goals. Instead, we can transform or transmute our difficult emotions into the gifts they bring. In fact, if we choose to approach every experience as an opportunity, we can see the gift that even greed may offer. The first gift of greed may be the chance to see that our abundance isn't outside of us. When I healed my thoughts on worthiness, money flowed to me from expected and unexpected sources. David always says to me, "Money is your energy," meaning our energy is the valve allowing receiving to happen. I have personally observed people in my life push away amazing opportunities because they were afraid. They were worried about how they were going to be able to fulfill a contract or whether they could deliver on their promises to clients. I'd observe them feel overwhelmed at the prospect rather than excited. Not surprisingly, for some reason or other, the contract would fall through. One of the best pieces of advice I received was to say "YES" and figure it out later. We may be pushing opportunities away right now because we feel overwhelmed about how to take the next step.

The second gift of greed could be generosity. This may sound paradoxical, but when I became aware of the behavior of people who were trapped by their money, I realized that hoarding isn't the way to the true abundance mentioned earlier. As illustrated by my story in Chapter 4, *The Universe Does Not Like a Vacuum,* money, like everything else, is energy. And energy wants to flow. When I'm generous with my money <u>and</u> feel good about sharing it, I'm signaling to the Universe/God/Source that I have more than enough to share with others. Additionally, sharing with others gives us safety. If I can be of assistance to you today, you may be more likely to assist me when I'm in need. Creating a community of people that love and support each other will ensure that everyone in our community is taken care of.

♥ Heart Stretch: Close your eyes, and relax your entire body, beginning from the bottom of your feet all the way to the top of your head. Breathe in and out three times to keep your attention on your body. Now focus on your heart and rest your hand there. From this place, answer these questions:

- *Which one of the walls of separation are you giving your energy to?*
- *Do you envy others?*
- *Do you hoard money rather than share it generously?*
- *Are there other walls of separation not mentioned here that are keeping you from connecting with others?*

Remember that the purpose of this exercise isn't to judge ourselves. Rather, it's to be honest, to approach our feelings with curiosity and love, so we can get past these difficult emotions. The seed to change is in the awareness of it. Those having a difficult time might try the compassion break introduced in Chapter 4 or another compassion meditation.

Hierarchy of compassion

I once read an article discussing the Canadian Parliament's arguments explaining the detainment of undocumented children. [4] The authors were able to show how compassion rhetoric was used to justify the detention of undocumented families. The authors explain the existence of a hierarchy of compassion whereby some people are lower on the rung of the ladder. Those we deem a personal threat to our lifestyle and livelihood are considered less worthy of compassion than ourselves. Politicians justified the detention of children by arguing that the real criminals were those bringing the children over illegally and that the undocumented families posed a threat to North American rights. Thus, the detention was presented as a compassionate approach to one group over another. It was also considered a deterrent to smugglers, although I'm not sure whether this has been effective.

When we view ourselves as victims, we can rationalize almost anything that may be hurtful to another person. At work, this is reflected in how we treat certain employees over others. Some are regarded as toxic, lazy, and reactive and not always afforded the same benefits as other employees without these seeming traits. For example, they might be overlooked for promotions, not treated with respect when they have complaints, or may be gossiped about.

Why do we justify being compassionate to some people and not others? Fear causes us to be triggered by something someone says or does. Beneath that trigger are unmet needs and limiting beliefs about who we are and who other people are. Often there's a belief that someone has power over us and has the ability to take something from or do something to us. What is not often clear, as mentioned earlier, is that we *give* others power over ourselves. Everyone is a mirror of us, telling us exactly who we are in the moment. This doesn't stop when we're at work! Our colleagues and our leaders mirror back our limiting thoughts and beliefs about ourselves, which is why we're sometimes triggered by our colleagues' behaviors.

Though the compassion rhetoric has often been hijacked by the veil of deservedness, Pema Chödrön elegantly reminds us that true compassion is between equals.[5] This means we're all fundamentally worthy and deserve all good things. But we're also human and have the potential to be hurtful as well as loving. Choosing whether to act in a hurtful or loving way is a choice we must make, and even people who make a negative choice at one point can always choose another path at any moment. The fact that those who are hurtful are not so different from any of us is important. Only when we have seen and accepted our own darkness can we see and accept it in others.

> ♥ *Heart Stretch*: *Close your eyes, and relax your entire body, beginning from the bottom of your feet all the way to the top of your head. Breathe in and out three times to keep your attention on your body. Now focus on your heart and rest your hand there. From this place, answer these questions:*
>
> - *What if instead of being a mirror for people's worst traits, we could be a beacon of light and see everyone as their best, most powerful, most beautiful, and most loving selves, even if they choose not to act that way?*
> - *Do you believe this is possible? Please note this can only happen when we first do it for ourselves; otherwise, we go into denial about who we and other people are.*

Punishment as a deterrent

When we're hurt, we may feel a need to punish. Perhaps during our childhood, we learned that punishment is the way to correct behavior. However, punishment leads to isolation, denigration, degradation, and separation from our fellow human beings. The recidivism literature shows that jails are not a proper deterrent and that offenders tend to reoffend. There are many reasons for this, but the clearest one from my perspective is that punishment does not teach someone the behavior they could aspire to. Jails merely surround people with others holding the same beliefs, energy, and vibration. Jails reinforce victim consciousness.

In the workplace, punishment may look like immediate termination, transfer to a less desirable position, or a constricting work plan. You may be thinking, "I don't punish people," but through your energy, you may be negatively contributing to the world by thinking negatively of others or by constricting your love toward others. While it's true that you can't harm another unless they agree to the alignment with your vision of them, you may be assisting their alignment with a negative experience.

♥ *Heart Stretch*: *Close your eyes, and relax your entire body, beginning from the bottom of your feet all the way to the top of your head. Breathe in and out three times to keep your attention on your body. Now focus on your heart and rest your hand there. From this place, answer these questions:*

- *How do you react when you are hurt? Do you withdraw your love and attention from the person? Do you not speak to the person for days?*
- *Do you get physically angry or verbally hurtful? Do you think negatively of the person?*
- *Now flip it: how do you want to be treated when you are hurtful? Do you desire to receive the same treatment you give?*

Please remember to observe this with curiosity and nonjudgment.

Chapter 8

A Return to Ourselves

It's not who you think you are that holds you back.
It's who you think you are not.
~ Anonymous

If love and compassion are our most natural state, how do we return to ourselves again? Psychologists have conducted numerous studies on how beliefs impact performance. In one such experiment, teachers were led to expect enhanced performance from certain students, even though none of the children was actually gifted. Researchers found that the teachers tended to rate the children they perceived as gifted higher because they believed they observed higher performance. This phenomenon can be attributed to the Pygmalion or Rosenthal effect, in which high expectations lead to improvements in performance.[1] Children who have been told they're gifted or highly intelligent and children who have been told they're not intelligent or are told they're not smart end up behaving differently.

The experiment tells us a lot about how we can shift our beliefs and, therefore, our experience. Could our compassion for others increase if we believed we were truly compassionate, more than we think we are? What if we believed we had a greater abundance of resources than we do? Then, we might be more likely to help others without the belief that it would tax us or hurt us.

Reimagining others

In this book, I have mentioned the need to reimagine how we work. Still, you may have noticed how I have been talking about the possibility of reimagining ourselves and others by changing our beliefs and emotions. Our experience of reality is based on what we think and feel about everything we experience every day. In order for us to have different experiences, we must be open to believing and feeling differently.

Reimagining others and our experiences together has helped me tremendously[2]. In Chapter 11, I share a story of how reframing an ongoing conflict with a colleague helped me resolve the conflict. But the most effective example I have seen of reimagining others is offered by Father Greg of Homeboy Industries. Father Greg and his colleagues dared to reimagine gang members as loving and compassionate people worthy of a better life. Father Greg's willingness not to get caught in society's definition of people who participate in gang life has resulted in incredible outcomes for people formerly involved in gangs. Through love and compassion, many gang members have been able to transform their lives for the better.

However, sometimes our reimagining doesn't work out the way we hoped. In the case of Father Greg, some of the gang members continued to choose a life of crime, but that doesn't negate all the people that have been helped by this approach.

People may not always act the way we desire them to, but remember that reimaging others is about who we're choosing to be and what we're choosing to align with. When I reimagined the people in my life, I found that either they aligned with my vision or they left my reality.

Still, we often find it difficult to reimagine people. We may prefer to see others as perpetrators in order for us to play out the role of victim. But when we no longer see ourselves as victims of others' behaviors but conscious creators and choose to accept responsibility for how we feel and think, we no longer need other people to behave in a particular way.

I usually like to reimagine events at night or early in the morning, when I'm the least resistant because my mind is calm. I don't know whether the circumstances change because I feel different and, therefore, act differently or whether I align with a different vibrational reality where that person is different, but the outcome is the same: somehow, my reality shifts.

I have done meditations where I imagine the circumstances as I'd like them to be, and I talk to the people involved in a positive way. First, though, I address any difficult emotions that come up for me personally. For example, when I was teaching, I had an issue with a student who was upset about their mark. I emailed the student explaining how I derived the mark and then went on holiday. It wasn't until I returned that I found the student's response in my inbox, and they were very agitated. The student was even more upset than before I wrote my email. My mind immediately went to the worst-case scenario. I was in fear. Would

I have to talk to the Dean and explain my marking scheme? Would I have to change the mark? How would that impact other students? Knowing that my fear could only align me to a worse scenario, I took a deep breath. I expressed love and compassion for myself first and then reassured myself that everything would be fine. I also decided to express love and compassion to this student and offered to take time out of my schedule to hear them out. I reminded them that they were important to me and that I was willing to listen and understand. I went to bed that night, deciding that no matter what happened, everything would turn out for the best. I imagined myself and the student being happy with the outcome. This helped me shift out of fear and helped me have a great night.

I didn't hear from the student until a few days later when they said they understood, and that everything was resolved. No need to meet. They also were compassionate toward me and wished me the best. In many other situations, I have been able to reimagine circumstances toward more positive outcomes and have found that events do magically turn around.

When facing adversities, the most loving and compassionate thing we can do is allow people to be and to see them in the best light possible. Telling them how they should change is usually met with resistance. Loving them and seeing them as perfect allows them to see it in themselves, as illustrated by my friend Tony. I have observed people's behavior completely change when I chose to see them as loveable and worthy. And even if they chose not to change, I chose not to be impacted by that. I chose not to be weighed down by expectations which may lead to resentment.

> ♥ *Heart Stretch*: *Close your eyes, and relax your entire body, beginning from the bottom of your feet all the way to the top of your head. Breathe in and out three times to keep your attention on your body. Now focus on your heart and rest your hand there. From this place, do the following exercise right before bed:*
>
> - *Think about a person or situation you find challenging. I suggest that the first time you do this meditation, you pick a situation that's only mildly challenging to you.*
> - *What emotions come up for you when you think about this person or situation?*
> - *Allow your feelings to arise. Where do you feel these emotions in your body? Do you feel them in your belly or in your heart? Send that spot love.*
> - *Ask yourself what you need in order to be able to release your resistance. Give that to yourself.*
> - *Now, imagine a scene where the event has a more positive outcome. Do not force it. The greater the force the more resistant you will be to the idea. You want the idea to feel natural. Allow yourself to encounter the more positive feelings of the event being resolved naturally and with ease. Fall asleep in those positive feelings.*

> *If you have a hard time getting into those feelings, that's okay.*
> *Just allow yourself to feel whatever comes up without a struggle.*
> *If you still can't, don't worry. Try again another day.*

Compassionate listening

Two approaches that have helped me be my most compassionate and loving self are compassionate listening and compassionate speaking. Years ago, I'd communicate in a way that focused on being right. With every word the other person was saying, I would be mentally creating my verbal armament, becoming impatient as I waited for the opportunity to offer my amazing counterargument. I wasn't having a conversation; I was having a debate. To truly listen, I needed to be willing to change my mind and heart.

What is compassionate listening? It is being fully present with someone, without judgment, and fully trusting that what they tell us is truth. Compassionate listening requires a willingness to understand their perspective from a place of love. I remember when I'd have arguments with my husband, during the time when I wasn't exercising my trust in others. He would share his perspective, and I'd go mentally, "Hmmm, no, that's not why he is doing this or saying this . . . what about x, y and z?" In my mind, I'd list evidence that was either for my argument or against his perspective. One day, most likely tired of our conflict, he said to me, "You can choose to believe me or not . . . that is up to you." In that moment, David made a decision to release his resistance to my lack of trust. Since there was no tension coming from his side, this allowed space for me to reflect on how I was contributing to the interaction. I was surprised, that this time, he wasn't going to try to convince me or prove his point. This helped me become aware that my "go-to" was not to trust what he was saying to me, even though David has never given me an indication he is anything but trustworthy. From that moment, I chose to take what he said at face value. Valerie Kaur, author of *See No Stranger*, has said the following: "Deep listening is an act of surrender. We risk being changed by what we hear."[3]

Compassionate listening requires us to fully witness the person in front of us as they are, instead of choosing to run a script in our head about who we've supposed them to be. This can be liberating for both sides as we re-know the other person and ourselves as well. The intent of compassionate listening is to bring us closer together. To look for commonalities, not differences. It is about opening our hearts and listening with our whole being. People are more wonderful, and more loving, generous, thoughtful, and interesting than we give them credit for, and we only observe this once we're willing to see it in them. Compassionate listening is about being in the energy of openness without the need to be right. Being right doesn't even come into play.

Silence plays a key role in compassionate listening. Too often, we listen with our response ready in the proverbial chamber, ready to be fired as soon as the opportunity arises. Often, when I'm challenged, I take the opportunity to breathe and focus on releasing resistance. I say to myself, "I release this resistance so I may receive the gift available in this moment." Not surprisingly, I get much more out of my interactions with people. Listening more and speaking less usually results in a deeper and more healing conversation than I was expecting.

Compassionate speaking

I was once observing a conversation between two people that wasn't going well. Both were in resistance and didn't feel heard, nor was either person listening to the other. A question arose inside of me. What if fear of rejection was behind all conflict in discourse? Did the need to be right have more to do with our need to feel valued and to belong? For example, if I'm wrong, maybe I'm not worthy or valuable.

When I'm having a conversation and the other person gets defensive, I try to ask myself, what's my true intention? Is it to be right, to be kind, or to share my knowledge? Is this conversation feeding my ego or feeding my soul?

Compassionate speaking is about sharing your truth in a way that doesn't disengage with or shame the other person. When I'm in conflict with someone, I find it important to acknowledge what I'm feeling. Once I have given myself compassion and love and validated my own feelings, I allow myself to acknowledge what I may need from the other person. I now begin difficult conversations from a place of giving the other person the benefit of the doubt, especially if they're challenging me. I will begin difficult conversations with, "I know it's not your intention to do x, y or z, but the impact of the interaction was this for me." With this sentence, I'm ensuring that the person maintains their dignity (if they choose to), and I'm assuming they're a compassionate person. Why? Because I care about them as a fellow human being and because that's who I choose to be. It doesn't matter if they intended the hurt or not. At the same time, I'm acknowledging that my feelings matter and are important, regardless of the intent. This allows me to release the need for the other person to validate my emotions and feelings, as I have already done that for myself. I then open myself to a conversation that enables growth on multiple sides.

Compassionate speaking is also about focusing on not saying hurtful words. It is imperative, though, to acknowledge that the words have no power in and of themselves. If someone insults us in a different language, it doesn't mean anything to us because we don't understand what they're saying. We give words the power to hurt us or to influence us by giving the words meaning, which can cause us to react to what others are saying. That said, it gives me pleasure to focus on speaking in a way that isn't disengaging and that acknowledges the divinity in other people. Does it work all the time? No, because I'm not always centered all the time. When I'm resting in my inner calm however, this approach is successful in helping me communicate with others.

Compassionate speaking is also about asking the right questions. Every day, I learn to ask clarifying questions instead of making assumptions. I don't always get this correct, so sometimes I will say, "Stop me if this doesn't resonate with you." In the past, if a person's response didn't match what I assumed, I figured they were lying. I'd point out all the words they had said in the past, like I was the word police. This again, was while I struggled to trust people and wanted to ensure I wasn't going to be duped. When I released my need to catch people and focused on believing what they said to me, the conflict in communication relaxed. Even if the person was lying, I realized that I need not be harmed by it. In fact, now, when I believe in the best version of people, they usually either try their best to live up to my hype or prove quickly why they don't deserve that belief. Compassionate speaking takes courage, however. We have to be willing to support ourselves through difficult emotions, both our own and those of the person we're speaking to.

For both compassionate speaking and compassionate listening, it's the energy behind the approaches that does the work. If we're only half listening or if we're listening with judgment or saying the right words but the energy isn't there, the other person will perceive this. Being honest with ourselves about our intent in the interaction is always helpful. If our intent is to be understood, then our goal must be to understand the other person. Since we're all connected, it helps to give others what we want to receive in return.

> ♥ *Heart Stretch*: *Try this loving kindness meditation for yourself and others adapted from Germer and Neff's* Teaching the Mindful Self-Compassion Program *(2019).*[4] *Close your eyes, and relax your entire body, beginning from the bottom of your feet all the way to the top of your head. Breathe in and out*

three times to keep your attention on your body. Now focus on your heart and rest your hand there. From this place, bring to mind someone in your life to whom you would like to extend more compassion. It could be yourself or someone else. See a vivid image of them in your mind. Allow love to emanate from your heart toward yourself or the other being.

Say the following phrases silently:

- *May you (me or we) be safe.*
- *May you (me or we) be happy.*
- *May you (me or we) be healthy.*
- *May you (me or we) live with ease.*
- *May your (mine or our) hearts be filled with loving kindness.*

Repeat this as many times as you want. You can also switch up the phrasing to "I am, or you are, or we are" and include other good wishes, such as abundance, joy, and peace.

Chapter 9

Redefining Power and Strength

Mastering yourself is true power.
~ Unknown

In REDDIT, the ANTIWORK thread describes workplace environments full of toxicity, bullying and harassment, power over approaches, and racism. Some posts report how workers were called in during already approved time off. When they refused, they were told that the manager was justified in retracting their vacation approval because someone didn't show up and they were therefore needed at work. The request usually ended with "Come into work or else." Clearly, the manager was wrong to attempt to coerce the employee to return to work after already approving their vacation request. But how many times, when we're in a situation where we feel we desperately need something or someone, have we used the same approach?

This approach stems from the fact that we have completely misunderstood what true power is. We idolize those who use power over approaches to push others into doing their will or who take energy from others and disregard the quiet power of silence, nature, and calmness. True power is effortless. To me, truly empowered people don't need to disempower others. They understand they're enough (worthy enough, loveable enough) and know they can create or align with whatever they desire. These powerful people understand that true creation comes from within, and they give themselves what they need in moments of struggle. Truly powerful people don't give away the power to determine how they feel about themselves. They stand in their own authority and don't give power to words and beliefs they don't want to experience.

People who need to control others are not in their true power and authority. The conquerors of the past, the colonizers, the oppressors were not truly powerful though they gave themselves systemic power. Jesus, Gandhi, and Martin Luther King Jr., whose legacies include peace, love, and compassion, are now understood for their incredible power. The conquerors are being seen for what they have always been, people choosing fear and lack. Many have suggested that conquerors were merely greedy, but greed is a belief in fear. It is a belief in never having enough, which is why they colonized others and took from them what they wouldn't willingly give.

The concepts of power we have grown up with and subconsciously reinforce, such as coercion and control, are examples of force, not power. In the same way, physical power means we use effort to move something heavy, but moving something with little strain or effort on our part is true power. Force is resistance, and when we resist something, we give it energy.

Trust and courage

As a child, I was taught not to trust. I was taught that people were dangerous and wanted to harm me, so we needed to put into place systems to prevent people from being bad. Even family wasn't to be fully trusted. I walked around with permanent armor on, not letting hurt in but also (unbeknownst to me) preventing love from reaching my heart. Worried about betrayal, I'd tell myself stories about people's intentions. It amuses me now to think I used to hold debates in my head about what I'd say or do if someone betrayed me or was hurtful to me, as if somehow that would remove the sting of betrayal.

I didn't realize then that I was perpetuating and increasing the likelihood of being betrayed because I couldn't allow true connection. I was also harming myself with my negative thoughts, like Don Quixote fighting invisible foes. When I was at my most vulnerable, I understood I wasn't afraid of betrayal but rather of the possibility I'd be unable to cope with it. At that point, I decided I was more powerful than I was giving myself credit for and worked on releasing my identity of victim to betrayal. I allowed myself the courage to trust. I can't control the behavior of others, but I can choose what I align with.

Trusting others is actually about trusting ourselves. When I gave others the benefit of the doubt from a place of allowance, they almost always proved me right. When I was placing my attention on what I feared, me choosing to trust didn't work. From trust comes freedom, too, because when we trust ourselves, we're free to love, free to give, free to be ourselves. When we trust others, we free them to be as they are because we don't need them to act differently. Often when we trust people, they step up to the plate. When they don't, we can have a conversation with them, with love and nonresistance, about what does not work for us. If people betray our trust, that speaks more to where they are emotionally and what we're both aligning with.

Trusting also frees us from the need to control others, which takes a lot of energy, time, and focus. Sometimes the most loving thing we can do for ourselves and other people is to love them from a distance. For leaders, releasing the need to control people gives them and their staff more freedom to create from a place of vision and imagination.

Trusting requires courage, especially if we're used to giving in to our fear-based beliefs. And the more we desire to trust, the more the fear in our minds will attempt to stop us. Every time I faced my biggest fears—death, disease, abandonment, poverty— my mind told me they'd come to fruition and be catastrophic. However, when I faced those dragons, they dissipated. They were nothing but clouds. I had to be willing to breathe into my fears, soothe my worries with trust in myself, and stand boldly in front of those fears in order to overcome them.

What does being with your fears look like exactly? When a fear comes up for me, I allow the emotion to arise without the need to judge it. I welcome it like I do any friend bearing news. For example, when I'm angry, I allow myself to feel those emotions because there's usually an important message behind those feelings. If I'm angry with someone, it might mean that I'm feeling disrespected or that my boundaries have been overstepped. In this case, my anger may reflect a need for me to support myself in reinforcing my boundaries more. My anger sometimes hides deeper feelings, such as sadness or disappointment in myself, if I feel I allowed someone to take advantage of me. Usually reassuring myself will allow the anger and sadness to fade away. If I can't find a way to soothe the anger, I allow myself to express it physically. I let out my anger in a safe container by punching a pillow or my punching bag. Then I will use my compassionate voice to remind myself that I'm safe. That I'm loved. That I'm enough. Sometimes, I hold an image of myself as a baby. I speak to that baby about her big emotions and tell myself what I always wanted to hear as a child. When the emotions feel too big, I give myself time and choose to face them another day. I will also ask myself, "Whom in my circle of love can I reach out to? Who will give me what I need in this moment, when I can't offer it to myself?" and wait for the message in my heart. This always leads me to the person who has the perfect message for me in that moment.

> ♥ *Heart Stretch: Close your eyes, and relax your entire body, beginning from the bottom of your feet all the way to the top of your head. Breathe in and out three times to keep your attention on your body. Now focus on your heart and rest your hand there. From this place, reflect on your relationship with trust and courage:*
>
> - *What am I most afraid of and why? What do these fears keep me from doing?*

> - *What do I believe about trust and courage?*
> - *Can I trust myself and my heart during the most challenging moments?*
> - *What can I do to have more courage and trust in my life?*

The power of presence

As I practiced courage and trust, I allowed myself to be more present in all aspects of my life. This reminded me of a thought experiment I did while studying for my MSW. I was toying with mindfulness and decided to completely immerse myself in the experience of listening and being with a person doing a presentation. I chose a person at random. I asked questions thoughtfully and placed all my energy on what the student was sharing. After class, I completely forgot about this experiment until one day many months later. The person who did the presentation came up to me and said, "I still remember how thoroughly you listened to my story ... you must be a good therapist." I was stunned. Though it didn't take much effort for me to be fully present for another person, this small gesture had a powerful impact on them, one that lasted for months.

We can always tell when someone is truly present or not. Their energy is either turned toward us or away from us. When they have turned their energy away from us, they feel distant, distracted, and may not remember what we said or what they agreed to. On the other hand, when people have their energy turned toward us, we can feel seen, acknowledged, appreciated, and feel important, even if the person doesn't do anything intentional or physical to prove it. That same presence can be turned inwards toward ourselves. Being mindful of our own thoughts and feelings and how we're creating, without judgment, can help us feel seen and heard. Many of us were deprived of our parents' presence because they were preoccupied or in fear, and we may have interpreted this as our being unworthy of their attention. At times, I felt like I was waiting to see the real me, to acknowledge who I really am, and to then allow myself to express that to the world.

When we're present with ourselves, we gain an appreciation and a willingness to be there for others. Sometimes this has unexpected payoffs. But don't take my word for it. My sister, Jessica, an in-home nurse at the time, told me that seeing the humanity of her patients helped her connect with their needs. Surprisingly, treating people with kindness, dignity, respect, and love also led to them sharing their deepest secrets. When we approach people without judgment but with a desire to witness them, they feel witnessed. They feel safe enough to be vulnerable with us.

To be truly present in our personal and professional lives, we must first attend to our own emotional needs. Fear of the future or pain from the past keeps us from being present. The present moment is where our power lies. It is only in this moment that we have the capacity to be fully present for ourselves and others. This can feel challenging, however, because we're surrounded by distractions.

Doing versus being

In a world where we have been taught that action is the key to success in all endeavors, silence and inaction are usually met with resistance. Taking action feels akin to having power and control over a situation. The more action we take, the more powerful we must be! But as seen in my manifesting example in Chapter 4, I attended a number of job interviews and got nowhere until I let go of my resistance. When I reflect on the experience now, I see that I could have reached the same destination with less effort. In fact, exerting a lot of energy is quite ineffective if not properly harnessed.

I prefer instead to take inspired action when something excites me or makes me feel good. The excitement is how I discern if the situation will turn out well. When I take inspired action, I usually get the best and most successful outcomes, bringing me closer to my dreams. How do I know the action is inspired? It makes me feel good, especially after I have completed it. The good feeling doesn't go away later.

But taking inspired action is not common.

Long ago, my passions tended to be associated with achieving something: "I want to revolutionize child welfare" or "I want to build a global company."

David's dreams, however, were about being: "I want to live a life of joy and travel and shine my light to the world for others."

At first, I didn't understand his perspective. In a world where we glorify ambition and doing-ness, he didn't seem to have dreams at all, which frustrated me. Now, however, I see the great wisdom in his perspective. His nonattachment to how his desire was to be fulfilled has led him to be that shining light for others under varied circumstances.

More and more, my definition of work is changing. My creations (how I refer to my work) are about my being. I see them as an extension of myself, of who I am. I desire to create and be of service without attachment to outcome or need.

In North America, we have a culture of "overwork." We glorify the grind. We think it makes us special and wear it like a badge of honor. In mysticism, though, quiet inaction is often more powerful than action. Quiet, silence, calmness, and presence allow us to align to our good more than forced misaligned action ever could.

Here's an example of how the belief in action lead an organization to abandon a helpful strategy.

I was attempting to bring mindfulness and meditation practices to one of my workplaces but had met with some resistance. The staff had interest in practicing mindfulness due to the high level of stress, but some leaders were understandably worried about the optics. Despite all the evidence-based benefits of meditation and mindfulness practices, I was still told that "the government doesn't pay people to sit around." While I was surprised by the reaction and may even have judged it at the time, I have since become aware that I wasn't great at "not doing anything." It took me a long time to realize that resting is just as necessary as action. Resting, relaxing, and being still, give us the resources we need to spring into action when the time is right. In my manifestation experiences, releasing and allowing have been the most important things I have done to enable the greatest good to come into my life. What happened in my organization? In the end, we did implement a mindfulness practice, and it was very well attended. However, it was not maintained because we all got too busy.

> ♥ *Heart Stretch*: *Close your eyes, and relax your entire body, beginning from the bottom of your feet all the way to the top of your head. Breathe in and out three times to keep your attention on your body. Now focus on your heart and rest your hand there. From this place, reflect on your relationship with doing nothing:*
>
> - *Think about what it would feel like to do nothing at all. No laundry, no cleaning, no emails. Nothing, except what you enjoy.*
> - *How do you feel about doing nothing?*
> - *Whose voice are you hearing? Allow the discomfort to sit with you.*
>
> *Now if procrastination is an issue for you instead and you are good at distracting yourself, it's because you may be afraid of getting it wrong. Instead, I invite you to go into your heart, ask it what baby steps you can take to take inspired action, and then take that action! You can always come back to this exercise after you read the section on reframing failure on Chapter 15.*

The transformative power of love

We discussed earlier how people come to believe in conditional love and what that may look like at home. In the workplace, conditional love is more innocuous. If you are a good worker or unproblematic, you may be liked, praised, or promoted more than if you are not. We also love clients who are polite, supportive, and understanding. But we have no idea what people are facing in their personal lives and why they behave the way they do until we choose to become curious instead of judging them.

Love is by far the strongest power that exists in the Universe. Because love and fear can't hold the same space, when we choose love, we allow ourselves to get out of alignment with our belief in fear. This gives us the power to transform the most difficult circumstances into something that can be healing for ourselves and others. My friend Rukiye Abdul-Mutakallim is a beautiful example of a person who chose love over anger and hate. She chose to stand in her true power.[1] You see, Rukiye's son was gunned down and left for dead by three people, two of them under seventeen, for $40 and take-out. She was lucky that her son didn't die on the spot, and she was able to say goodbye to him. During the trial, Rukiye realized that two of the people who killed her son were merely kids. Rukiye chose to become curious about what led these children to commit such a heinous crime. What she learned from listening to the story of those young people was that there was a long history of trauma in their families. From this space, my friend could forgive them for murdering her son. The video of her hugging one of the young people and his family has gone viral and has been watched at least 40 million times. Rukiye chose not to allow hate and anger to destroy her and the people around her.

Because Rukiye understands the interconnection among all beings, she now focuses her attention and energy on addressing unresolved trauma. Every day, she helps people work through their trauma and lack of self-love. Every day, she saves the lives of other young children like her son and the people who harmed him.

Not allowing external circumstances to change you, destroy you, or veer you off your path is true power. To look on the shadow of humanity and be able to find love for it and not let it change you. Truly powerful people lift others up through their presence. Of course, my friend does not believe her son is truly gone, either. In her heart, she talks to him every day.

♥ *Heart Stretch*: *Close your eyes, and relax your entire body, beginning from the bottom of your feet all the way to the top of your head. Breathe in and out three times to keep your attention on your body. Now focus on your heart and rest your hand there. From this place, answer these questions:*

- *Has your perspective on power changed?*
- *Can you think of an experience where something that seemed negative was transformed into something positive?*
- *When you think of Rukiye's story, what thoughts and feelings come up for you? Allow yourself to feel without judgment.*

Chapter 10

Changing Our Consciousness to Change Our Work and Our Lives

If we all worked on the assumption that what is accepted is really true, there would be little hope of advance.
~ Orville Wright

"You're trying to change the reflection," David said to me, frustrated. We were chatting about my perceived lack of success in my business. "You have to change yourself, and the reflection will change. The world outside is an output."

"I know, I know," I replied, frustrated, too, wanting the conversation to end.

It feels like, in life, we're all trying to change the mirror. We are so disappointed with the systems we have created and the lack of love and compassion in the world we live in, but we desire others to change so we can experience what we desire, not realizing that our beliefs, emotions, words, and actions are aligning us with what we don't want to create every single day.

Start where you are

"It all begins in the home," said my friend Rukiye, as she explained to me how she forgave the young men who shot her son and left him to die. She told me that every day, people are playing out their traumas in life and at work, traumas that began in their childhood. "Many people are held hostage by the people in their own homes due to trauma," Rukiye reminded me.

In the beginning, I thought she was talking about addressing traumas and conflicts with the people in our lives. I decided to talk with people I knew who held diametrically opposed perspectives to mine, like Trump supporters from the Latin American community. I have since written a blog about it, but, essentially, we chatted about our differing viewpoints without the desire to change each other. What surprised me most about the conversations was that these people were not extremists but rather held a completely opposite perspective from my own. They desired the same things as I did: to be heard, seen, supported, to be free and accepted regardless of differences. I noticed more united us than separated us. None of us changed our viewpoints, but listening to one another without judgment definitely brought us closer. Neither side felt they lost anything.

As I was writing this book, I realized Rukiye was perhaps alluding to something even deeper than I originally had assumed: the fact that each of us must clean up our own inner home. We have to clean up our emotional signatures—our energies and vibrations—to better focus on what we want to create, not what we want to repel. We then have to love ourselves and be kind to ourselves on the journey to realizing our dreams. The first step toward this journey begins with our thoughts and feelings.

Acknowledging our identities

The majority of us have had experiences that caused us pain, whether it be abuse, loss, or grief. Sometimes we have labeled these experiences "traumatic" because they still cause us suffering. According to the Canadian Centre of Addictions and Mental Health, trauma is a "lasting emotional response that often results from living through a distressing event."[1] When I think about the distressing events I have experienced, I realize that after the experience ended, it was my own suppressed emotions and negative thoughts that kept re-traumatizing me. I experienced pain, but my resistance to feel the emotions and my resistance to avoid being hurt again caused me more suffering and created my trauma. I was suppressing the emotions by distracting myself or avoiding feeling altogether. Instead, I had to learn to see these emotions without judgment, not as something wrong. This was uncomfortable and scary. But I held on to the idea that freedom lay on the other side of my fear, so I kept showing up and showing up.

I also had to accept where I was in my journey. Only then was I able to move more easily to compassion and love toward myself. Looking at the reflection, as David calls it, without attaching to what I see, but taking it as confirmation of where I have been, had helped me ease my need for control. It also allowed me to become more aware of how I was creating my own reality by the identities I was embodying.

In my healing journey, both personally and professionally, I have discovered that my trauma led to the creation of specific identities. Over time my beliefs about my powerlessness and the emotions that accompanied those beliefs drew me to create habits that contributed to a vision of myself as a "victim." We don't realize this, but when we focus on the perpetrators of whatever experiences we have had, we're also reinforcing our own identities as their victims. This is what we call victim consciousness.

You would be surprised how often we subconsciously reinforce these identities and rehash stories of our own brokenness. Every time we say, "What's wrong with me?" or "X broke me," we're reinforcing our feeling of powerlessness. Instead, I suggest asking ourselves where our power is in any moment. This doesn't mean we ignore our pain. It just means that in our darkest moments, we'll be able to see the light.

It was challenging to view all the identities I'd created for myself: victim of trauma, over-giving mother, co-dependent spouse, fearful and anxious person, overachiever. All of these identities played out every day in my life and at work. It is so interesting that we have created work environments where we're encouraged to leave our emotions at home when it's absolutely impossible to do so because our identities and the thoughts, beliefs, and emotions attached to them travel with us wherever we go. Our identities reflect our core thoughts and our emotions and behaviors. I currently don't support any stories of myself or anyone else that reinforce an identity of victimhood.

The reason programs that only target behavior don't work is that they seek the lowest level of change. In order for us to permanently change our behavior, we have to adopt a new identity. For example, we have to shift from identifying as a "weak" person to a "strong" person. To change our identities, we must change our core thoughts and feelings. We do this over time when we create new habits. New habits become subconscious, and they then become part of who we are[2]. The illustration on the next page demonstrates the different levels of change that can occur. This diagram was inspired by the work of the incredible Frederick Dodson[3] and his five levels of reality creation.

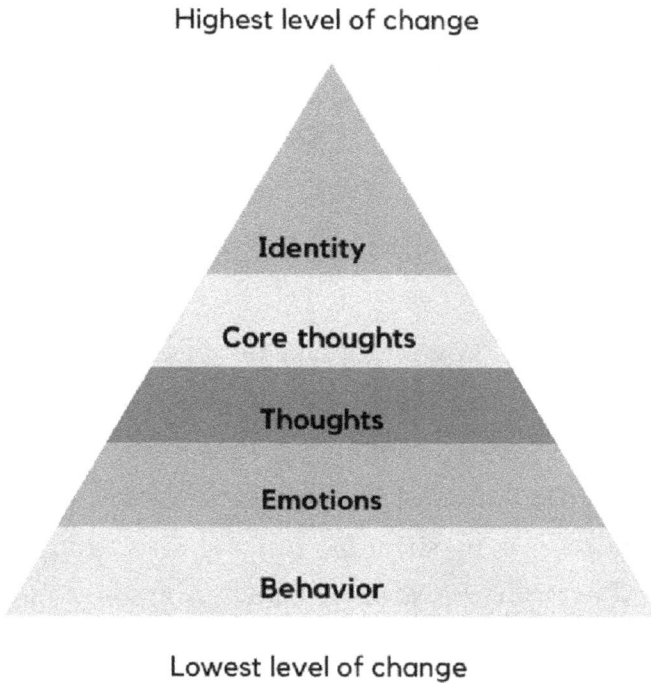

Highest level of change

Identity

Core thoughts

Thoughts

Emotions

Behavior

Lowest level of change

Figure 2. Levels of change

Please note that these levels of change are never linear. They act synergistically, and people flow in and out of different levels at different points in their lives. In order to understand this, reflect on the following example:

Suppose we want to be wealthy but are currently poor. If we decide to change our wealth status at the lowest level of change, at the behavior level, we'll take actions to be wealthier: save more, invest more, or purchase lottery tickets. However, this level of change is never long-lasting. Even if we win the lottery, if we don't change our poverty mindset, we soon end up poor again or poorer than before. The second and third levels of change usually interact together. People who are poor may have a hard time getting out of poverty if their beliefs and emotions are poverty based. Sometimes reframing that poverty as just an abundance of lack can be helpful in helping us shift out of poverty consciousness.

I should note, however, that I'm not victim-blaming. We have created systems that unfairly disadvantage some groups over others. However, even though it's not our fault, it is our responsibility to offer ourselves the best possible outcome within the systems that exist by changing our alignment and supporting ourselves. We can do this while also addressing the consciousness that has led to us to create a world where income inequality exists.

What I mean by offering ourselves the best possible outcome is this: If we're in fear every time a bill comes or if we constantly worry about losing money or not having enough, then no action we take to change our wealth status will be helpful long term. However, if we change how we feel about the bills and approach them from a more positive perspective, we'll be able to make changes to our circumstances. Even if we pay the minimum monthly payment for a particular bill, we can do this with gratitude. The energy of gratitude then aligns us with other circumstances that increase our potential to be more grateful.

It is also important to note that limiting thoughts usually have core beliefs embedded within them. For example, we may have core beliefs of not deserving abundance or may have a negative view of people who make money and thus may not be receptive to wealth even if we believe we truly desire it. Once we identify these core thoughts, we can change them. Then all smaller thoughts and emotions will align, leading to changes at the behavior level. We will start to see more opportunities all around us and be more receptive to different ways of making money, and we'll take more inspired action.

Changing at the highest level, the level of identity, results in long-lasting change. It can also be the most difficult approach because it means we now see ourselves as wealthy. We are in the energy of wealth. We like to spend time considering what we do with our wealth. This doesn't mean we overspend or go on crazy shopping sprees we can't afford. Instead, we do a mental exercise, or we visit stores we would never go into and just browse. It is about being in the energy of our wealth. When circumstances arise that don't reflect what we embody, it doesn't shake us. We pay our bills with joy at the thought of paying the bills. We understand that these reflections are old energy, and we keep our attention and energy focused on feeling wealthy instead. Embodying wealth usually results in extraordinary things occurring, such as opportunities we didn't see before or money that comes to us from unexpected places. Embodying our new identity means we're no longer the same person we were before. The old identity that was poor seems like a distant memory, and we're now a wealthy person.

Where most people struggle is when their reality doesn't conform to their chosen identity. At this point, they might give up and revert to their old beliefs and emotions. When I was first starting out in my business, I wanted my success to be immediate. As time passed, however, and I got closer to not having any money after my savings had been depleted, I became more and more scared. I didn't want to admit it to myself, so I kept repeating and pretending that I was wealthy and that I was in the flow. However, every time something happened externally that didn't support my idea, such as an unexpected cost, my thoughts went negative, and my feelings were deep fear. These thoughts and feelings demonstrated that I had not embodied the wealthy person I wanted to be. They showed me who I really was when these circumstances arose. When I began truly seeing myself as wealthy, the bills came, but they had no impact on me. I looked forward to paying off my mortgage and all my bills with gratitude and joy. I also learned an important lesson from this experience. Constantly monitoring for change only reinforces that we're not what we desire to be—that's why we're looking for it. The different levels of change can be used for anything: weight loss, relationship issues, or anything else we desire to happen. I encourage you to try it out for yourselves.

> ♥ *Heart Stretch*: *Close your eyes, and relax your entire body, beginning from the bottom of your feet all the way to the top of your head. Breathe in and out three times to keep your attention on your body. Now focus on your heart and rest your hand there. From this place, answer these questions:*
>
> - *What are the identities you mostly align with every day? How do your daily habits reinforce these identities?*
> - *What identity would you rather embody instead? What do you think it will take for you to embody this change?*
> - *What thoughts and emotions come up as you imagine your new identity? Allow these thoughts and feelings to arise with curiosity.*

What do I need?

When I saw myself as a victim of my circumstances, I was never fully aware of how much power I had at any moment. The habit of asking myself, "What am I feeling right now?" and "What do I need?" helped me to embody a new identity. This exercise also allowed me to gain greater awareness of how many needs I had allowed to go unnoticed and unaddressed. I understand, of course, that this approach can be challenging when our needs have been suppressed for a long time. If it's challenging for you, try the exercise below instead.

Why was I constantly checking in with myself? In order to move beyond my previous identities, I had to give voice to the emotions that underscored them. I sought to understand what I needed in every moment to offer myself what I was looking for externally. I knew that I would not be able to move toward embodying my new identity as successful until I addressed the fear underneath my identity of "failing." Addressing the fears helped me shift my thinking from negative to a more positive mindset. If you want to learn how to become more aware of your own needs, try the exercise introduced at the end of Chapter 4.

> ♥ ***Heart Stretch****: Close your eyes, and relax your entire body, beginning from the bottom of your feet all the way to the top of your head. Breathe in and out three times to keep your attention on your body. From this place, start to listen to your heart.*
>
> - *Our friend Susan Pollock, author of the book,* Self-Compassion for Parents, *taught me the effective strategy of looking at things with our hearts.[4] First, open your eyes and examine your hands. What do you see? Take a good look.*
> - *After examining your hands, close your eyes, and place your focus on your heart. Open your eyes and try to see through your heart. Now look at your hands. Do you still see them the same way?*

Mindfully dealing with negative thoughts

"How can I stop my negative thoughts?" someone said to me when I hosted a talk on loving ourselves more deeply. We were discussing choosing loving and compassionate thoughts instead of fear-based thoughts.

"Well," I said, "it takes practice. You have been practicing negative thinking, catastrophizing, and scaring yourself for a long time. It's going to take you showing up for yourself every day, practicing more positive thoughts and facing those fears as they arise."

It can take time to develop new thoughts and beliefs, which then turn into new habits and eventually a new identity. Awareness of our negative thinking is the first part of the journey. In order to gain greater awareness of my negative thinking and feeling, I had to be more present. This is similar to the impact that being present for others has on them. When I became more present, I became more aware that I was constantly either in the future or in the past. I wasn't living fully present in any moment and wasn't living a joyful life.

Mindfulness, or present moment awareness, is a key aspect of being loving toward yourself and others. Mindfulness helps us gain awareness of what we're thinking or feeling and who we are being at a particular moment. In my own practice, mindfulness helped me realize how I was bringing the thoughts and dramas of the previous day into the following days by reliving any related fears in my head. When I acted the same way to the same stimuli, day after day, I was reinforcing its reality in my life[5].

Although mindfulness is becoming mainstream, it's important not to lose the purpose of mindfulness practices. The true power of mindfulness lies in bringing us back to ourselves and to the point where we have the most power, which is in the now. Mindfulness has also helped me get the most joy out of the present moment. It helps me realize the beauty and wonder that exists in our world that I was missing. It also helped me to understand that all the things I feared were in some possible future. A possible future that was not set and was part of an infinite number of potential futures. None of what I worried about was happening at the moment when I was worrying about it. Worry and doubt take away our enjoyment of the present.

The gift of mindfulness is also being in the flow. When you are feeling a positive emotion and marry that with a state of relaxation—which occurs only when we're in the present moment—that opens us up to receive more. We are in the flow in the present moment because we're no longer resistant to how things are. One way I like to stay mindful is to do things I enjoy. I play games with my children or go for a walk in the forest. Nature is a great way for me to come back to myself.

To understand where our attention is in a given moment, we can ask: who am I being right now? Not what am I doing but who am I being? This gives us greater awareness and allows us to choose something different. Am I in some possible future? Is that possible future negative? Or am I in the past? Are any of the events

I'm thinking about happening right now? Once we become more present and get back to our power, we can begin to choose the thoughts and feelings we want to have. We can examine all areas of our lives and start to be more conscious creators in our world.

I find it fascinating that many people apply spiritual and growth approaches in their lives but fail to make the connection in their workplaces or in business. Sometimes, they'll use manifestation approaches to create their business but not to attract and hire the perfect people or to resolve workplace relationship issues. When we think we can be affected by another person, we play out the identities that we believe are appropriate for those beliefs. In order to change our experiences, we have to discover the identities we're playing out, understand why we're playing them out emotionally through our negative thoughts, and then make a new choice.

In all my years in the workplace and in doing consultation work, I would always hear that the culture of an organization depended largely on the energy or attitude of the boss/CEO/owner. That's because we give or defer our power to people who are in charge. If we all stopped doing this, that person would no longer have all the power in an organization. But sometimes, we're more comfortable deferring responsibility to other people, especially if we don't desire or are not ready to take responsibility for our own lives and success. Eventually, however, people will get tired of this and choose to change.

The cost of not changing

I believe that the COVID-19 pandemic mirrored to us our need, as a collective society, to change ourselves. Given how much strife, fear, and discord are present in the world, we can no longer afford not to change. We owe it to ourselves and to others. The collective conflict is rising, however, to be healed, not to make us retract or feed more fear. Now is the time to choose whether we want our personal lives and workplaces to look the same or to look vastly different.

In my life, however, I have observed that individuals would rather stay the same rather than choose to change. Many believe that changing takes too much effort and only choose to change when the cost of remaining the same is greater than the cost of changing. It may take a seemingly negative catalyst like an illness, a job loss, or a divorce that leads them to finally make a change. At this point, I believe we have reached a critical mass in consciousness now whereby change is inevitable, and choosing not to change will only result in more chaos.

Chapter 11

Taking Our Power Back

I can be changed by what happens to me,
but I refuse to be reduced by it.
~ Maya Angelou

Growing up, I had a voracious appetite for learning. I wanted someone to show me the way, to tell me what to do, to walk me hand in hand to the beautiful life I'd envisioned for myself. I'd learned from many spiritual teachings that "When the student is ready, the master will come." But what happens when the master does not come, or rather, as David says, when you have to step up and be the master yourself?

"At some point, you're going to have to stop looking for guidance outside of yourself," my husband said when he saw me scribbling copious notes from my favorite book on mastery.

My attachment to learning had to do with my fear of embracing my own mastery. I didn't feel I knew enough to fully support myself. But his comment made me reflect on my ability to attain mastery while still identifying as a student.

No one is coming to save you

We have the power to create our dream life, right now. However, we often defer our power to other people: experts, coaches, researchers. We attribute our success to others, but what actually causes our success is a change from within. Having worked as a coach, I believe that my job is for my clients to free themselves from needing me as quickly as possible. I'm like a guide who offers one map to their destination. There are many maps they can use, but inevitably, they have to walk or drive themselves to their goal.

Sometimes we worship the map or the guide rather than trusting ourselves to get us to where we want to go. Worshipping others is disempowering because we believe they're above us. They are not. We are all made up of the same Source/God and have the same abilities even though we look different externally. Sometimes people get so hung up on approaches they fail to recognize that there's no magic bullet. No single approach can work for everyone because each of us is on our own journey and need to listen to our inner guidance

I have always been a cautious person, one who learns from the mistakes of others. In contrast, some people must make mistakes in order to learn. Neither path is better. They are just different.

When I examined what helped me change from an anxious, untrusting, catastrophic thinker to an empowered, calm, joyful, and trusting being, I realized it was showing up for myself, every single day, and doing the work. What work, you ask? The work of overcoming my attachment to my fears and choosing loving and positive thoughts every time; the work of going inward when I faced challenging circumstances and trusting the God/Source/Universe within me in those moments. Sometimes, it was incredibly hard. Other times, I floated through life in what seemed to be a happy daze—only to be triggered by something small and innocuous. *Crap,* I said to myself, *I thought I'd dealt with this.*

At first, I'd beat myself up for being in the same spot as I'd been before. But I got better at responding lovingly to myself when I tripped over the same rock. I got better at laughing at myself and my behaviors and reminding myself that I was NOT in the same spot as I was before. I was aware this time and could choose differently. But I still had to make a choice. I couldn't be both a victim and a master of the situation.

What do you want?

Now, when I'm coaching people on how to live their dreams through greater self-love and self-compassion, one of the first questions I ask is this: If there were no barriers, what would you be doing? In other words: What do you really want? You'd be surprised how many people can't answer this question. Some give me excuses as to why their dreams can't come true. They actually list the reasons. They're already defeated before they begin their journey. They want the people in their life to change or their circumstances to change so they can be happy. But I'm not interested in changing other people; I am interested in understanding the dreams of the person I'm working with so that we can focus on aligning reality with those dreams. When we're clear about what we want, and when we don't waver from this vision, the Universe lines everything up.

Some people don't know what their dreams are. They say they have to get back to me. How can we go after what we want if we don't know what we desire? For this reason, many of us settle at work and in our personal lives.

I understand this perspective, of course. If our choices or desires were judged by someone important in our past as something that was either useless or pointless, we may believe we don't know what we desire as a shield to avoid criticism. If we're not used to getting our needs met, we may not ask or may not know how to ask in the first place. For those who have no idea what they desire, my advice is this: follow your joy or bliss. Ask yourself: What makes me excited? What makes me happy? If these questions are too hard to answer, start smaller: What do I like to do? Do more of that.

Remember that visualization isn't limited to the dreams we want to create. We can also extend it to the people we want to meet. Some folks list characteristics of their dream person and end up meeting that person. I'm one of those list creators. And this power isn't limited to our personal life because our work life IS our personal life. We can use this visualization to meet the perfect accountant, employee, employer, and so on.

*♥ **Heart Stretch**: Close your eyes and relax your body beginning from the bottom of your feet all the way to the top of your head. Breathe in and out three times to keep your attention focused on your body. Now focus on your heart and rest your hand there. From this place, revisit the bold dream you had in Chapter 2.*

- *Is it as bold as it could be? Could it be bolder?*
- *What do you want? What do you really, really, want? I'm not asking you what you think you can obtain; rather, what's the biggest, boldest, most "out there" dream you have?*
- *If there were no barriers, what would you be doing?*
- *What are you passionate about?*

Our attachment to fear

Another excuse I receive is "I don't have time to do the things I want to do, because I have to work." We can always carve out time for what matters even if it's as little as ten minutes a day. People who use the time excuse are inadvertently saying that their dreams are not important. If we were told when growing up that what we liked to do was a waste of time, we may be more likely to prioritize responsibilities over what we want to create. But once we invest in ourselves and do what we love, we discover more and more things we love because of the law of resonance. Things that vibrate at the same resonance are attracted to each other, so the more we do what we like, the more things we like will be attracted to us. I've heard the saying "wealthy people invest in assets, whereas poor people invest in liabilities."[1] There is no greater asset than ourselves.

All of the excuses we tell ourselves are based in fear. Fear is a tricky thing. When is it friend, and when is it foe? Growing up, I believed that my fear could prevent me from getting hurt. However, fear didn't help me during challenging situations; it was my own inner compass, my heart, and my own inner strength that helped me get out of jams. Most of my fears were anticipatory—fear of things that never came to pass.

I used to think my fear itself was what kept me small, and armed, putting a stop to my dreams. My fear, I thought, made me hurt because when I was in fear, I overreacted to stimuli and ended up hurting both myself and other people. It's interesting now observing how much we believe fear can imprison us. In fact, fear is a belief just like everything else. As David says "It does not occur outside of the mind." What gives fear power is our attention to it.

Fear often spreads like a virus because people don't stand in their own authority. They will defer to the most powerful energy and accept it instead.

But resistance to fear isn't the answer because resistance keeps fear alive. We often assume we're in resistance when we say to ourselves, "I don't want this." The key, though, is the emotions that accompany this statement. If we feel angry, upset, fearful, constricted, then we're in resistance. If we're in denial, we're in resistance too.

Fundamentally, when we resist something, we believe that the thing we fear has power over us. This is a different feeling from allowing and then choosing what we desire to experience. The thought *I don't want this* may be the same, but the feeling will not be. If we believe something has no power over us, we'll acknowledge that we perceive it and then choose to believe and feel what we desire instead. The feelings that accompany what we desire to experience will be ease, joy, relief, and happiness.

Please note that I'm not recommending that we ignore resistance when it arises. Instead, allow it, accept it, love it, and release it in order to choose something that feels better. In the next chapter, I'll speak more about resistance.

Reimagining my reality, at work

When I was working in management, I struggled with a colleague who took everything that came out of my mouth personally. This was already a particularly challenging time at the company, and I was new in my role. I felt things needed to change, so I was eager to get in there and offer my perspective. In retrospect, my "help" must have been seen as criticism by one of my colleagues, because they reacted negatively almost every time I asked a question or made a comment. Perhaps there was an element of judgment underneath my eagerness to improve my organization. Needless to say, this person's reactions to my input were often harsh and angry. By the nth defensive reaction, I pegged them as resistant to change. I was tired of the way my intentions were immediately shot down.

By this time, I had enough experience with self-compassion and self-love to understand that I'm never powerless under any circumstance. The first thing I did was ask myself, "Okay, where is my power in this moment?" I knew I could only control how I reacted to the situation, so I decided to get curious about why I was reacting this way. What immediately came up for me was: "Oh, I'm not feeling valued!" I was new to the job, so their reaction triggered the story "I'm not worthy . . . I don't know what I'm doing." Not feeling valued was a long-standing issue for me. I'd never felt truly heard and seen as a child, which was why I was triggered by my colleague's reactions. Once I realized what was going on, I could soothe my worries: "Of course, I'm worthy and valued . . . I have this new amazing position, and look at all the incredible things I've accomplished. My value doesn't decrease because someone doesn't see it."

After I gave myself what I expected from my colleague—nurturance, validation, support, reassurance—I got curious about them. I decided to use a compassionate lens and give them the benefit of the doubt. I chose to believe the following:

- They were doing the best they could, as was I.
- They were not trying to hurt me. They were a compassionate being who cared about people, me included.
- There was something going on for them when I made a comment, and I needed to understand it.

When I shifted away from the perspective of being a victim (or even a perpetrator, if you see my eagerness to help as judgment), I wondered if they felt judged by me. What I discovered, after chatting with them was that they were feeling helpless about what was happening in our workplace at the time and were unsure if they were "doing what they were supposed to do." They were also not feeling valued. From then on, I made sure my communication was conscientious and not based on assumptions. I focused on asking how I could be of assistance rather than suggesting what I thought should happen and reminding them of their team's amazing accomplishments. My default setting became giving people the benefit of the doubt. This led to positive changes in our interactions and in the relationship.

Does this mean that I became the workplace Mother Teresa, Buddha, or Jesus? Not exactly. We never know when we're going to be triggered by the way someone behaves, so compassion is a choice, I make DAILY. Practice is imperative until we embody compassion and curiosity. We must practice approaching situations from an understanding that life is a mirror of us. It all starts with ourselves. I had to address my own emotions and get them out of the equation; only then could I hold space for the other person. When we're in the throes of deep feelings this isn't the time to try to understand the perspectives of others. Once we allow ourselves the time to soothe and nurture our own hurts, then we can get curious about other people.

Going back to my experience with my colleague, when I changed my mindset about them, their behavior toward me changed too. It felt like magic then, but now it makes sense. She was mirroring what I was feeling internally. To reimagine her successfully, I had to be willing to go inward, acknowledge the emotions I felt, and validate them. I needed to soothe those emotions with support, kindness, and love and then get curious about the other person's intentions, feelings, and beliefs. I had to shift out of my dualistic thinking and focus on what made us more similar than different.

Later in life, I'd encounter the work of Neville Goddard, who suggests we should revise our days and the people in our lives to let go of our old stories of ourselves and others. What do I mean by "revise our day"? Allow yourself to mentally see your day as you wished it had gone rather than as it happened. This exercise will allow you to start the next day anew. Revision also helps us release some of the most challenging emotions that come up during our interactions with others.

♥ *Heart Stretch*: *Close your eyes and relax your entire body beginning from the bottom of your feet all the way to the top of your head. Breathe in and out three times to keep your attention on your body. Now focus on your heart and rest your hand there. From this place, try this exercise to reimagine someone or something that may be challenging for you:*

- *Begin with curiosity for yourself. Where is my power in this situation?*
- *What am I feeling? What do I need right now? Soothe yourself with love and compassion.*
- *Get curious about the other person or event. What is really happening here? What might others be thinking and feeling?*

- *Choose the identity you want to embody and act from this place toward yourself and the other person.*
- *Continue to offer yourself compassion during your difficult emotions. Rinse and repeat.*

I suggest trying this on smaller issues first rather than facing a big issue without practice. You'll avoid encountering a lot of resistance and giving up altogether.

Chapter 12

Releasing Resistance

Pain that is not transformed is transferred.
~ Richard Rohr

Growing up I was always fascinated by the story of the Wright Brothers. They looked up at the birds in the sky and thought, I can do that. They dared to think about something that had never been accomplished before and to believe they could do it. They had to hold on to that vision every single time they crashed.

The concept of flying is still bizarre to me. Planes weigh between 30,000 and 127,000 pounds. The fact that only lift, weight, thrust, and drag are keeping them in the air is a miracle of engineering! How could we put our mental effort into creating something so incredible and yet not put the same level of effort and expertise into solving humanity's most challenging problems? How come we can go to the moon and fly but can't solve racism? Underneath this lack of desire to deal with the most negative aspects of our lives must be the belief that, while flying benefits all, having a more just, loving, compassionate, and equitable world does not. How did flying become possible in our collective consciousness when ending hate did not? How is it not something we all want?

When I was younger, I blamed systems for perpetuating our entrapment, for creating the circumstances that led to people being isolated, punished, and marginalized. Even our schools appear joyless. Like you, I might have also blamed leaders for setting into place systems that seemed so biased. Then I realized that these systems were mirroring how I acted when I was hurt and stuck in victim consciousness. When I felt the most powerless was when I'd strike out or hurt others the most. When someone was hurtful or if I was afraid of them, I wanted them to get as far away from me as humanly possible. Sending them to the moon was too close. I was afraid of people. I thought they wanted to take advantage of me or take something from me that I didn't want to give them. I wanted people who wronged me to be punished to prevent them from ever hurting me again.

However, as I took my own power back and practiced self-love, I realized that if others had power over me, I had given it to them. I'd unintentionally co-created a world with systems that act the same way I did when I was hurt. It's hard for us to admit we have helped to create a world where racism, rape, segregation, murder, fraud, and other problems exist. We want other people and systems to change; we don't want to change ourselves. But until we do, we're not going to experience a change in our outer environment. Not fearing others and not hating those who harm us are hard work. It is difficult to embody love and compassion. But every time we choose to isolate, hate, or belittle someone (anyone) we create the conditions that allow problematic "isms" to exist. If we're going to help create a better world, we must choose to embody love and compassion in every moment of every day. Will you make that choice?

> ♥ *Heart Stretch: Close your eyes and relax your entire body beginning from the bottom of your feet all the way to the top of your head. Breathe in and out three times to keep your attention on your body. Now focus on your heart and rest your hand there. From this place, answer these questions:*
>
> - *Will you maintain the current reality or have the courage to birth something new?*
> - *Are you willing to address your fear and treat it with love by showing up for yourself when you are most afraid?*
> - *Are you willing to trust yourself, trust life, trust God/Source/Universe when you are unsure?*

Resistance

Many of us have heard the saying, "What you resist, persists." It is common in compassion training. However, we fail to see just how much we resist in our daily lives. Every time we want to fight, hate, or oppose something or someone we're in resistance. Even denial is a form of resistance because denial is saying we don't want whatever we're looking at to exist. We pretend it's not there even though our feelings toward it don't change. We resist because we subconsciously believe the things we resist are permanent and unchangeable; we believe they can impact us. But they only have the strength we give them. By placing our energy and attention on what we don't desire, we inadvertently give those things power. Letting go of resistance or accepting that we've created something or contributed to something we don't like or want to accept enables us to focus on what we want to create.

How do we know we're no longer resisting something? By how we feel about it. When I experience something I used to be resistant to but no longer give power to, I can observe it and not be impacted emotionally. Recall the boat example: I chose not to drown with the people struggling to swim. I did this because I knew drowning with them would not help them get on the boat. I realized I had a choice about how I felt and what I wanted to create.

As I said in Chapter 4, we tend to place a lot of attention on programs to fight outcomes we don't like, such as racism and drug use. The same attention, energy, and resources would be better spent on finding solutions by focusing on what we do want to create.

♥ *Heart Stretch*: *Close your eyes and relax your entire body beginning from the bottom of your feet all the way to the top of your head. Breathe in and out three times to keep your attention on your body. Now focus on your heart and rest your hand there. From this place, answer these questions:*

- *What if resistance is actually an incredible gift?*

- *What if when we encounter it the most, we're closer to the next stage of our healing?*
- *Do you have the courage to face it and walk through it by allowing it to be?*

The need to be great!

Seeing the world in a rigid, right-and-wrong, black-and-white way is a form of resistance. A conversation I had with David helped me understand how my need to see myself as a good person was contributing to the story that others were "bad" (or, at least, not as good). We were chatting about my trying to bring compassion into the child welfare system, when he said to me.

"You're just playing the game of duality," David commented.

"What do you mean?" I asked. I'd thought my life's purpose was to bring greater love and compassion into the child-protection system, but I was meeting with a lot of resistance from the field in general. There didn't seem to be an interest in my perspectives, and the less interest I observed, the more frustrated I became.

"Well," David said, "These systems are dualistic because they pit one side against another. The system focuses on 'bad' parents or 'good' parents, or children's rights versus parental rights. It's all duality. The desire to change these systems and the individuals within them means feeding the duality that exists within these systems."

He spoke as if what he was saying was self-evident. "Go on," I said, but I rolled my eyes.

"To truly change these systems, you have to leave duality. You have to stop seeing aspects of them as good or bad."

He was right. Human beings see the world in a dualistic way: good versus bad, cold versus hot, up versus down. However, when we expand our view of life, we see that everything is connected and on a larger continuum. Winter and summer are but two seasons in the whole spectrum of nature. Cold and hot are but different degrees on a temperature scale. Good and bad and right and wrong are but behavior choices and perspectives on a continuum. But our collective dualism means we place everything we experience into the "good" or "bad" pile.

I hadn't realized that beneath my desire to be the hero of child welfare was an intent to force my ideas on others within the system and thus make them "wrong." I also hadn't realized that emotions such as love, compassion, and joy are balanced and don't have a true opposite. They can't be forced but are felt when we're in a state of ease and grace.

"It's all your energy anyways," David said as he left the room.

This conversation helped me reconsider my intentions. While it was true that I wanted to incorporate love and compassion into child protection to alleviate the suffering I observed in the families, children, and workers I interacted with, there was also an element of ego that was moving this forward.

When I sat with my own feelings, I realized that my self-worth was tied to this endeavor. As the child of a person who grew up experiencing terrible abuse and neglect, I most likely went into child protection hoping to rescue my mother and myself. I wanted a system that would have helped my grandparents be more loving toward themselves and their children. I also wanted the suffering my family and I had endured to mean something. Behind all these good intentions, there were also elements of desiring to be known, to be special, to be unique and different and separate from the whole. I had to be here to do something great! However, in those challenging moments, I could look at myself and ask: Can I still unconditionally love myself, even if I accomplish nothing? Even if I don't meet my goal of saving child welfare? Can I still accept myself, even if I lead a quiet life and don't change anything but rather accept everything in all its inherent beauty and perfection?

♥ Heart Stretch: Close your eyes and relax your entire body beginning from the bottom of your feet all the way to the top of your head. Breathe in and out three times to keep your attention on your body. Now focus on your heart and rest your hand there. From this place, reflect on your previous self-love answers:

- *What conditions do you place on self-love? Self-acceptance?*
- *Could you love and accept yourself just as you are, in this moment, without needing to do or achieve anything?*

David and I have had a lot of conversations about the dichotomy of good and bad thinking. In compassion work, we talk about looking at the silver lining, the good side of what's perceived as bad. But what if there's no bad? Or good? What if something isn't inherently anything except what we perceive it to be? A snake is neither good nor bad; the value placed on it is determined by the individual perceiving it.

The conversation I had with David that day, about my role in child welfare, also helped me see how my resistance was affecting my relationship with my fellow child welfare workers. Because I judged the system as wrong, I judged them as wrong for working within it. When I judged others, I opened myself up to judgment. However, when I moved away from the desire to judge, and the desire to force my own perspective on those working within the system, I could see where I could make a real contribution.

Realizing that I don't have to earn my own love by accomplishing anything and seeing possible failure as neither good nor bad have opened up my creative power so my creativity and joy can flow through. I thought relaxing my fears would lead to complacency. But what I found was just the opposite. If it weren't for that release in pressure, this book would never have been written. I'd been putting off writing a book because I felt everyone was writing one. What could I possibly contribute? When I released my limiting beliefs, I could enjoy the process of writing and write for myself.

Once I let go of expectations for myself to achieve or perform and allowed myself to enjoy the moment, I could also do that for others. When I think about my children's future, I don't think about them entering this or that profession. I think about them living joyful, abundant, and happy lives with the people they love. We so often place pressure on our children to perform because we worry about their prospects. I have full confidence that my children will do well no matter what they do.

Stuck in the victim story

Therapy helped me a lot in my journey, but over time I noticed a pattern. My therapists graduated me when I wanted to continue coming in. I didn't realize that my desire to keep talking to a therapist meant I was unwilling to let go of my story. I had a subconscious desire to stay stuck in the victim story, to hashing it over and over, to probe into my wounds, looking for the shadows and inadvertently reinforcing my lack of mastery. Unfortunately, I'm not unique on this. We do this because we believe it keeps us safe. When we're living with trauma, we get used to reinforcing our identities and their survival strategies. Challenging these identities feels uncomfortable.

One of the most powerful lessons I learned in my self-love journey was that we don't have to go digging for anything. As soon as we inject love into ourselves, the opposite will rear its ugly head and say hi. It's not our job to resist it, hate it, or admonish it. It's our job to continue to offer that ugliness love until it releases (or, as David would say, allow it to be experienced without attachment). But what we often do instead is go back to our old behavior that reinforces our victim story.

I believe our job in life is to free ourselves from fear and limited thinking as quickly as possible and step into our mastery. As I mention in Chapter 10 on changing our consciousness, when we change our thoughts and feelings and adopt a new habit of focusing on where our power is, we can begin to gain it back. How we accomplish this comes from within us. But what happens when groups of people are stuck in victim mode?

CRISIS environments

I was chatting with a friend of mine Susan Marie and telling her that my workplace was constantly in a state of crisis. She shared with me the following acronym for CRISIS: creating resistance in situations instead of surrendering.

Wow, I thought. That's right.

When I examined our crisis environment with a new lens, I realized that the resistance came from a lack of trust and fear of not having enough. Many of the policies and procedures, due to bureaucracy, had been created from a place of fear instead of discernment.

Sometimes, in business environments, when one or two people do something that is not favorable to the company, leaders rush in and create policies to prevent other staff from doing the same thing, rather than looking at themselves. Over time, these businesses create more and more policies, and the workplace becomes more constricting and fear filled. People who work for these businesses feel constrained and untrusted, and this creates a greater distance between the leadership and staff. Discernment on the other hand, means understanding why a person acted in a particular way and rewarding the other staff for not behaving in the same manner. We should reinforce behavior we want to see. When we try to prevent behavior we don't want to see, we inadvertently reinforce it.

Fear in the workplace hinders us from having love and compassion for others. Where fear reigns, love can't flourish. In 2011, C.D. Cameron and B. Keith Payne published a study on what motivates people to move toward or against suffering.[1] Compassion collapse occurs in those people who can't regulate their emotions when faced with people who require compassion. This is because they don't feel they had sufficient resources to help themselves, let alone others. In fact, Paul Gilbert, a top researcher from the United Kingdom, found that workers who have fears about compassion will consciously or unconsciously ignore suffering and abuse so that they don't have to address it.[2]

Drama mama

As a young girl I loved fruit, and Peru has the most delicious and decadent fruits I've ever tasted. I remember sitting down, mango in hand, and enjoying every single bite. Have you ever had such a fantastic mango that you enjoy every bite and keep eating it until the pit is bone dry? I have. Don't you wish we could live every aspect of our lives with the same delight as a child eating a mango?

We don't for two reasons. The first is victim consciousness. Sometimes people who are used to chaotic environments are uncomfortable in peace so they subconsciously create problems. This allows them to live out their identity as survivors and use the strategies that worked so well in those circumstances. It's a safety net of sorts.

The second is fear of the unknown. Growing up I heard the saying "Better the devil you know than the angel you don't." What a terrible saying! No thanks. I'd rather meet an angel any time than stick around with the same old devil. Of course, I'm joking. I don't believe the devil exists. The real message of this story is this: the belief that what we don't know may be worse than what we do know keeps us small.

What if what we don't know is exponentially better than what we imagined? In fact, many of the most spectacular things in our lives are unknown to us. For example, where did we come from? What are we doing here? How do we fall in love? If we're willing to face our fears of the unknown, we'll find there are worlds to explore even within our homes and definitely in our own hearts. There is more magic in the unknown than in the known. The known is where complacency lives.

♥ Heart Stretch: Close your eyes and relax your entire body beginning from the bottom of your feet all the way to the top of your head. Breathe in and out three times to keep your attention on your body. Now focus on your heart and rest your hand there. From this place, reflect on your relationship with drama:

> • *Do you love drama in your life? Do you find having a life of peace boring?*
> • *How might your identity be contributing to greater drama in your life?*

Shame

Shame is another form of resistance. According to Ely Garfinkle, the root of the word is "to hide."[3] Shame is one of the most insidious emotions we can feel. Shame makes us feel unlovable; it makes us believe that our mistakes are inherent traits. According to Brene Brown, guilt is different from shame: it involves feeling bad about something we've done, not about ourselves for being imperfect human beings.[4]

When I started doing compassion work, I worried that people would come out and say that I was a fraud or point out that I'd hurt people and that this would be proof that I was, indeed, unlovable. The truth is, loving myself beyond my own flaws was the kindest thing I could ever do for myself. Often, what prevents us from being truly compassionate is that we think we have to be perfect to embody love and compassion. Not so. Some of the most hurtful people can turn into the kindest, if given the opportunity. Difficult emotions like shame can be transmuted into greater self-love.

My experience with shame

I'm keeping the details of this event purposefully vague out of respect for the people involved. I'm including the important part: my personal experience with the feelings of shame.

There was an incident with a person, and I needed to decide how to address it. I didn't have much experience with the circumstances, so I deferred to others instead of discerning for myself how I should manage it. Although my gut told me I could do it different, I followed other people's advice and decided to be a good soldier. I hadn't realized until then that being a "good follower of procedure" was something I held in high esteem. This "good girl identity" led me to put belonging before following my own wisdom.

I scheduled a meeting with the individual and told them what they needed to do to move forward. Then I went on with my life. I wasn't aware that my interactions with this person had a horrible impact on them. They saw me as an oppressive force. You can imagine my surprise when I found out. Rather than validating their perspective and hearing their side of the story when we met again, I was caught off guard, got defensive, and made things worse with my response. I realized afterward that I'd become defensive because their perspective invalidated my view of myself as compassionate and supportive.

At one point during our conversation, I felt like I was outside myself, observing everything. I asked myself: What are you doing? When I calmed down, I saw how wrong I'd been.

Regardless of whether I agreed with their perspective, had I apologized and listened more, the issue could have been resolved. Instead, this person's perspective of me as a hurtful person was reinforced, and I left feeling shame and guilt.

Luckily, I was practicing self-compassion and meditation at the time. I allowed myself to experience the feelings of deep shame and reminded myself that I had not intentionally hurt this person. I reminded myself that I wasn't a bad person, even if I had behaved badly, and that the key to changing my behavior was examining where I'd gone wrong. I realized that in following protocol, I'd completely missed the human being in front of me.

Despite how challenging these emotions felt, I'm deeply grateful I had them. The incident taught me so much about who I was being and who I wanted to become. That interaction led to me devoting myself full-time to love and compassion work. When I look at the experience, with the eyes of love, I realize that I'm the villain in some people's stories and the heroine in others. But I'm neither. I'm just me, doing the best I can, hoping to be better, more loving, and more compassionate with every choice, failing sometimes, being successful sometimes . . . and always working toward greater love.

Allowing the chaos

"Compassion is allowing all things to be," David said as we were having breakfast. Now that we were self-employed, we took time out to have conversations about life and consciousness before starting our day.

I chewed and swallowed. "All things? What about crimes like sexual assault, racism, murder? Should we allow those things to be?" I felt uncomfortable.

"It's the resistance that keeps them in manifest," David said.

"I have to think about this one," I said. I switched to the topic of our children.

At first, I met this idea with defiance. I interpreted David's words to mean turning a blind eye to what's happening in the world. But knowing my husband to be a kind person, I understood this wasn't what he meant. Over time, I learned that allowing things to be meant focusing on nonresistance.

One of the most profound truths that helped me have compassion for myself and others is that we're spiritual beings with a physical experience. This means my soul and those of others can never be hurt beyond repair. Since I believe everything was created by one Source/God/Universe, this also tells me first that we're all divine—and remembering the divinity in myself helps me remember the divinity in other people.

In my experience, God is love; God is endless understanding and patience. Once, during a meditation, I felt an incredible sense of love from within me. I got a glimpse of what it must feel for Source to look at us. I felt such an incredible awe for humanity and realized how beautiful, perfect, and amazing we all are. "I can see why you like us," I said. The feeling emanating from my heart made me chuckle. From that larger viewpoint, I saw that the Source within us experienced us as magical because we're an extension of itself and, thus, unbreakable.

This experience helped me see that the Devil doesn't exist, or rather that the devil is a human creation. Evil is a choice we make. By the same token, it's also a choice we can unmake. Marianne Williamson's famous poem, "Our Deepest Fear," speaks to our hearts because our inner selves know it to be true.[5] We are more powerful than we give ourselves credit for. However, I think we also know that we have misused this power, and that's why we may be afraid. All the negative things in our lives—disease, vermin, death, rape—all of them were created by us. We have used our God-given power to feed and grow fear rather than to create a dream world for all. Why did we do this? I believe it's because somewhere along the way, we lost the connection with ourselves and one another. We forgot our true power. We became small, weak, fearful, and we created more and more walls of separation. Allowing the chaos doesn't mean ignoring what's happening. It's important for us to acknowledge to ourselves what we, as a collective, have created. This will help us realize that this chaotic world isn't what we desire, and it will help us understand what we need to do within ourselves to choose differently.

Does saying "we align with the chaos in our lives" mean I deserved or purposefully caused the pain that happened to me? No. I would never have consciously chosen to hurt myself or others. However, minimally, I can say I'm responsible for how I reacted to that pain and those events. I'm responsible for continuing to hurt myself with my negative and catastrophic thinking.

Understanding that I was no longer a victim of external circumstances but a conscious creator of my life helped me shift away from fear to love.

> ❤ *Heart Stretch: Close your eyes and relax your entire body beginning from the bottom of your feet all the way to the top of your head. Breathe in and out three times to keep your attention on your body. Now focus on your heart and rest your hand there. From this place, reflect on your relationship with allowing the chaos of life:*
>
> - *What comes up for you when you hear "compassion is allowing all things to be"?*
> - *Can you see how allowance may be helpful in releasing resistance to the things we don't desire to create?*
> - *Do you believe we're more powerful than we give ourselves credit for?*

Chapter 13

Workplace Leadership

Two things define you: Your patience when you have nothing and your attitude when you have everything.
~ Imam Ali

Did you ever dream of working in a place that was your destiny, a place where you thought you'd grow old and change the world with your amazing work? At one time, I did. This company—let's call it Company X—had a reputation for high-quality work, and that work related directly to my dream: helping children who suffered maltreatment.

When I went to work for that company, I thought I'd hit the jackpot. I'd been dreaming of it for at least five years and got the interview by cold calling and being at the right place at the right time. The owner and I were the only ones who trekked through a terrible snowstorm to attend the interview. It seemed like the whole universe had conspired to ensure that I was the only candidate present that day. "You're hired," he said enthusiastically.

I'd love to say that soon after that all my dreams came true, but they didn't. I discovered the unhealthy work habits that troubled this workplace. I managed a large project at multiple locations and a staff of over twenty with little support. My manager asked for unreasonable timelines. They wanted updates on everything within five minutes of making a request, even when I was doing payroll for my team because someone had quit suddenly. I was doing the work of three people, I felt. My ideas were shut down, and I was "told" what I should be doing. My manager even asked me for my email password when I was off sick one day and they needed something done.

Meanwhile, staff were quitting like the building was on fire. My colleagues and I talked about how bad we were treated and how hard it was for the company to retain staff. Overwhelmed by the endless demands, I applied to different positions and went to work for another organization. I left the project before it was complete because I just couldn't cope. The most disheartening part was that once I began the new job, I realized I'd forgotten how to think for myself. Having been told what to think and micromanaged, I didn't have any ideas of my own. When I asked my new leader (who ended up becoming a mentor) what to do when a challenge arose, she said, "I don't know . . . what are *you* going to do?" Her fresh leadership and belief in my abilities, even when I didn't believe in myself, helped me return to my most empowered self.

But let's return to the story of Company X. Once I received confirmation I'd been hired elsewhere, I spoke to the manager to help them understand why I was leaving and why the turnover was so high. I assumed the manager wasn't aware of their own behavior, and I hoped awareness would lead to a change in the workplace so they could retain good people. I didn't want to leave the job; I was leaving the management style. I came into their office and decided to be honest with them about the reason for my departure.

"I'm leaving because I'm severely micromanaged. You micromanage me in everything I do." I already had another job and had nothing to lose.

"You're micromanaged because I'm micromanaged." They said barely looking up from their computer.

Their answer shocked me. This manager was as miserable as I was, but rather than address the issue with our mutual boss, they chose to stay silent, stay in fear, and pass on the oppression to others.

"Well, that's a miserable way to work," I said. I felt somewhat sorry for them.

They nodded.

Treating our employees with compassion

Traditional styles of leadership focus on force and coercion. These styles are often seen in environments where people are treated without compassion and respect. I believe we're letting go of the last relics of traditional leadership. That's why we're seeing a rise in fear and the desire to control from those who still use these methods. Leaders who use this approach can sometimes become addicted to using coercion and control. It can feel good to have people do exactly what we want them to. However, so long as a leader derives their power from outside themselves, they'll continue to use these approaches. If you remember from Chapter 9, true power comes from within.

Companies that focus on maximizing their profits by oppressing their workers and paying them the bare minimum don't make sense. Why? Because most large companies require staff to make them successful. They require workers to do the work of running the business. Workers are the company. If leaders acknowledged the enormous value that workers bring to the table, they'd treat their employees like gold. One of the best Ted Talks I've seen is by Derek Sivers, "How to Start a Movement."[1] The talk is about the value of the first follower. Sivers gives the example of someone dancing alone at a festival, whom he compares to a lone nut with a great idea. The first follower is the first person who believes in the nut's vision and helps accomplish it. Without these followers, the vision can't come to fruition.

Companies have been able to oppress people because the people working for them are focused on their fears. What if the company moves to another country? What if I don't have work? If every company moved out of a country and there was no employment, that would cripple that economy because no one would have purchasing power. But no effective government is going to allow a whole country to go into a deep recession without supporting their people. Remember that, from an energetic level, "the universe does not like a vacuum so when something leaves, something comes in its place." There is no loss in the universe except what we believe.

As a society we're finally getting to the point where people are fed up with being treated oppressively at work. People working in toxic environments are tired of some people making maximum profit while offering staff little compensation. The more companies treat their staff with love and compassion and pay them abundantly, the more they'll see huge rises in profit and will succeed during times of great upheaval. Why? Because people will no longer be willing to accept anything less than the best treatment at work. Plain and simple. Because of this, I believe that over time we'll see a huge shift in how we do business.

In my mind, people are loving and compassionate and don't want to work in an oppressive environment, but they can't get past their belief in lack. They believe this is the only way for them to succeed. But there's another way. Once we address the fear, the energy can be used most productively. Then we can align to our unlimited abundance while supporting the abundance of others.

Fear versus empowerment

Back at Company X, my manager couldn't express compassion for me and my suffering because they were suppressing their own suffering. They left Company X a few years after I did. Of course, I now realize that micromanagement comes from a place of fear and lack of trust that everything will work out. People who need to control every aspect of their lives do so because they can't internally regulate. They need everything outside of them to be perfect, or they'll dysregulate. Underneath it all is a belief that they won't be able to cope with whatever comes next. Truly empowered leaders regulate themselves first and trust that regardless of what's happening on the outside, they can master anything that comes their way.

Now it would have been easy for me to say that my former manager was a horrible and oppressive person who hurt me and many others who worked for them, but the situation was more complex than that. It usually is. Yes, they chose to behave in a way that was oppressive to their staff, but I also accepted that behavior. In fact, we all did. None of us said anything; people just left, and the cycle continued. We feared losing our jobs, so we tolerated more and more constriction and force.

Often, we remain silent because we're in the grip of fear. My fear caused me to accept behavior I wouldn't accept outside of the workplace. But the compassion and love I had for myself caused me to leave.

When I think back on it now, I'm grateful for the experience. It taught me good boundaries at work; it clarified what I didn't want to create and what I didn't want to accept in the workplace or at home. In fact, when I look back at my experience, I realize boundaries were an issue I was struggling with in my personal life, so of course, that experience would be reflected in my work life.

Although the experience was challenging, it allowed me to clarify my desires. In the next job, I made it clear that I didn't want to have the same experiences . . . and I experienced the opposite.

My new leader was compassionate, supportive, trusting, visionary, and willing to listen to me.

Power and workplace leadership

In the twenty plus years I was in leadership, I had both oppressive bosses and empowering supportive leaders. I must also confess that I've been both! I was the pushy, untrusting boss when I was anxious about timelines and deadlines or worried about outcomes. This behavior overlapped with when I was most unsure about my skills and abilities as a boss. When I was a compassionate leader, I fully trusted my abilities and those of my staff, and I knew in my heart that everything would turn out well—and it always did. I regulated my emotions during my most difficult moments.

Having been both types of leaders, I promise you that being a caring and compassionate leader produces results in a way that being an overbearing boss never can. Staff give 110 per cent when they feel valued, seen, and supported; they want to do the work. I've taken teams that were considered toxic and inefficient and assisted them in becoming the most functional teams in our agency. All I did, though, was allow them to see themselves as I saw them: capable, loving, intelligent, compassionate, and thriving. I genuinely loved seeing the staff step into their own power and become a team when I supported them and got out of their way.

I should note that I'm not speaking about servant leadership. Servant leadership is a leadership style where the goal of the leader is simply to serve the staff. Depending on how it's done, it can sometimes negatively impact the leader. I've observed leaders burn out because they focused solely on their staff's needs and then got angry at themselves because they had nothing left to give. Remember, it's imperative to put on our own oxygen mask before we assist others. Leaders who can't support themselves first, open themselves up for exhaustion or worse—to becoming reactive and hurtful.

> ♥ *Heart Stretch*: *Close your eyes and relax your entire body beginning from the bottom of your feet all the way to the top of your head. Breathe in and out three times to keep your attention on your body. Now focus on your heart and rest your hand there. From this place, reflect on your relationship with leadership:*
>
> - *What is your leadership style? Be honest with yourself. Don't judge where you are; just observe.*
> - *Where did you learn about power and leadership? Who were your leadership role models?*
> - *Did your leadership models come from your parents?*

Buying into others' stories

Most negative leader-staff interactions come from the stories people tell themselves about who they are and who others are. Often, I hear stories that paint others in a one-dimensional way: "She's toxic," "He's lazy," or "They're dishonest." These types of judgments lead us to treat people poorly. But in many cases, when I dug deeper, I discovered that the story was based on an incident that happened once in ten-plus years. When I suggested we have a conversation to address these beliefs, the leader was hesitant.

When we're unsure about whether we or someone we know is creating a story about another person, we can ask ourselves: Is this person spoken about in all-or-nothing language? Do they always or never do something or show a particular trait? As I mentioned earlier, we all have the capacity to be considered "good" or "bad." People are complex and beautiful to behold. Their reasons for doing something or not doing something always stem from some underlying core thought or belief. But we find it easier to think of people one dimensionally than to get curious about their intentions. But consider this: people always act in ways that makes sense to them. When David gets frustrated with something someone did that he can't comprehend, I joke, "Common sense is not so common."

Another story I've heard is that the organization needs protection from its own employees, as if the people working for the company were separate from its performance and success. This story leads to policies to ensure that workers are not taking advantage of the "business." To avoid creating a one-dimensional character of these workplaces, I can also say I've observed compassion and true concern for workers, and I've seen people rally together out of love and care for one another. But overall, I've observed a lot of workplace suffering, suffering that from my perspective was completely unnecessary, suffering that could have been addressed and managed in the moment by leaning into one another, having difficult conversations, and expressing mutual love and kindness. To quote Eckhart Tolle, "Suffering is necessary until you realize it is unnecessary."[2]

> ♥ *Heart Stretch*: *Close your eyes and relax your entire body beginning from the bottom of your feet all the way to the top of your head. Breathe in and out three times to keep your attention on your body. Now focus on your heart and rest your hand there. From this place, reflect on the stories you tell yourself:*
>
> - *Consider a situation you find challenging. Pick one that isn't triggering to keep yourself engaged in the process. Who are the players in this situation? Describe them as if you're telling the story to someone else. What stories have you told yourself about the people in this scenario, including yourself?*
> - *Now think about how you'd like to change the story? What outcomes do you want to experience with this person or these people? Be willing to reimagine them as you would desire them to be and be willing to treat them as such. If uncomfortable emotions come up, allow them to be without judgment.*

The energy of nonprofits

Throughout my career, I've worked for several nonprofit organizations in service of the most marginalized people. I never understood why not-for-profits were designed the way they were. They constantly struggle for money. In fact, I believe these organizations, especially those funded by the government, follow a nonsustainable model of care.

When the cost of living goes up (as it has during and after the pandemic), companies survive by passing on some or all of the cost to consumers. Consumers then ask for an increase in salary or raise their fees if they're self-employed. However, when nonprofits ask the government (or other funder) for money, they can only ask for an increase in salary for their staff. It's easier if they're unionized, but generally it's difficult.

The problem with the current model is budget limits or caps on government funding. In all my years working for nonprofits, governments cut budgets and asked staff to do more with less. This led to burnout, including in hospitals and child welfare agencies, which has led to strikes, quiet quitting, and the great resignation. With people now worried about whether their personal budgets can meet the increased costs of food and necessities, as well as their mortgage payments, no wonder people are spent—especially given their increased responsibilities at work.

Does this mean that organizations that care for the most marginalized should be for-profit or private? No. What I'm asking you to consider is how people who work in nonprofits can flourish. How can they work from a place of love, compassion, true care, courage, faith, abundance and openness rather than a fear of loss, death, austerity, and performance management? I'm talking about energy, not values. The values may be based on compassion and care, but the energy in these systems is often very different. I've observed compassionate people doing uncompassionate things because they were energized by fear of survival. For example, there was collaboration between community nonprofits but little pooling or sharing of resources because they were competing for the same limited government dollars.

To attract ongoing financial support, I suggest leadership and staff shift their energy from a deficit perspective to an abundance mindset. This will help them see more opportunities for funding from expected and unexpected places. Compassionate not-for-profit leaders can also discuss financial problems with staff. I've seen staff collectively decide to take days off (to temporarily shut down the company) to avoid layoffs. This strategy usually pays off, and staff can get the time and pay back. However, not all companies are in a position to do this, and not all staff be agreeable to because of personal needs. But the question should be asked: Can staff come together to collectively reimagine their financial situation? From an energy perspective, more bodies means more energy to fulfill shared desires.

The energy of nonprofits should also be aligned with acting in community. When we come together to assist one another, to help one another grow and share resources, we all benefit. But this takes work, commitment, and, most importantly, courage. We have to trust one another enough to take risks. We have to believe in our own abundance to the point that we don't think sharing with others will mean less for us.

If I could use one word to characterize my experience in these nonprofits, it would be CRISIS. That's where I was energetically—in workplaces that were in constant flux and hypervigilant. Staff were on guard and anxious. There was a lot of resistance to what was happening. When I became a leader, I learned the futility of being in constant fear. Treating everything as a crisis prevents staff from regulating themselves so they can see the best course of action. It also prevents us from being creative and taking risks. It prevents us from turning off fight-or-flight response. If we can't shift out of survival mode, we won't feel safe enough to be calm, compassionate, and relaxed, to be open to all possibilities.

> ♥ *Heart Stretch*: *Close your eyes and relax your entire body beginning from the bottom of your feet all the way to the top of your head. Breathe in and out three times to keep your attention on your body. Now focus on your heart and rest your hand there. From this place, reflect on the definition of CRISIS (see page 145).*
>
> - *How have you managed a crisis in your life?*
> - *What role did resistance play in the experience?*
> - *What helped you get through the experience?*

Chapter 14

When Things Go "Wrong"

Our beliefs about human nature helps shape human nature itself. What we think about ourselves and our possibilities, determines what we aspire to become and shapes what we teach our children both at home and in the schools . . . By encouraging us to expect the worst in others, it brings out the worst in us: dreading the role of the chump, we are often loath to heed our nobler instincts.
~ Robert Frank

Once, when I was talking casually with a colleague about leaving an agency, she said, "You know, we always know when someone has been fired." She laughed. "There's usually no mention of cake and a goodbye party in their email, so we call that the no cake email."

Oh boy, I thought, and tried not to show my reaction. I hadn't realized that the send-off for people leaving our organization because of performance issues differed from the send-offs for those leaving in good standing. This got me thinking about the importance of sending people off (no matter the situation) with compassion and respect. I wondered how we'd reached the point where we walked people out at the end of the day and expected them to disappear.

What happened to forgiveness at work?

Before we discuss how we manage terminations, we must talk about the lack of forgiveness at work. We handle forgiveness at work like we handle difficult conversations: we mostly avoid them. In some of my past workplaces, forgiveness was seen as a weakness that could make the leadership and organization vulnerable. Some of the companies I worked for had a one-strike rule for major issues and a three-strike rule for smaller behavioral problems. The three-strike rule wasn't always seen as an opportunity to understand the person's behavior and to forgive the trespasses but part of an evidence-gathering process to terminate with cause. In some organizations, noxious behavior was tolerated, again and again, but when it got worse, leadership moved to terminate.

I think forgiveness is challenging at work because of fear. Some of us are so afraid of being taken advantage of, or being a doormat, that we shroud our organizations with policies and procedures to control people's behaviors. We believe that if we're compassionate or forgiving, we're handing the other person an opportunity to take advantage of us again. How this looks in practice can vary. Some policies are so restrictive they don't meet the intended outcome. For example, school discipline policies focusing on zero tolerance often result in the suspension or expulsion of the child exhibiting a behavioral problem. But what has the child learned? We haven't taught them anything about how we want them to behave. The policy offers the child no support or guidance. Now, this isn't the school's fault. The zero-tolerance policy was created after public outcries that schools weren't doing enough to address children's behavioral issues.

Don't get me wrong. Sometimes the most loving thing we can do for ourselves and others is not allowing them to engage in a particular behavior again. Compassion for self and others requires healthy boundaries. But compassionate boundaries are flexible, based on curiosity and love. One rule does not apply to everyone, because everyone has unique circumstances. Compassionate boundaries require us take the time to fully understand each issue so we can address the situation in a way that works for all sides. Even if the person isn't ready to change, we can reimagine them in a more positive manner. We can forgive someone and release them with love. For our part, we can work on not allowing ourselves to align to the same experience again

I believe that nobody wants to be hurtful. The problem arises when a person believes that their own wishes or desires are directly tied to another person in some way and that the only way to attain their desires is to harm that other person. But once they realize they have the power to meet their own needs in a way that harms no one, the desire to hurt others ceases to exist.

As a society, we haven't gotten to the point where we can embrace the energy of forgiveness as a value. When I was hurt, I wanted to hurt others so they'd understand my feelings. I wanted to punish them so they'd never tried to hurt me again. However, this approach does not work. Following punishment, people rarely have a eureka moment that causes them to act in a fully compassionate and loving way from that moment forward. Punishment usually leads to greater distance between people.

On the other hand, when I'd hurt someone, I wanted to be forgiven, given another shot, to be seen as my true loving self, not solely as the person who committed the hurtful act. In my household, it's important to talk about behavior rather than who we are. For children in particular, talking about behavior implies it can change. Earlier, I mentioned that staff sometimes speak about certain people being toxic. I can only imagine how that must feel for the person being spoken about. We can point out people's toxic behavior without characterizing them in a negative way.

Finally, I believe our lack of forgiveness at work reflects a lack of forgiveness of ourselves. It's a mirror that should make us ask: How good are we at forgiving ourselves? I struggled with forgiving myself for the things I'd created or become aligned with, for what I thought was my fault, for what others did to me, and for what I did to others. Once I forgave myself for contributing to my own suffering, I let go of my need to forgive others. Looked at in another way: once I took responsibility for how I felt and decided to no longer let others have power over my feelings, then I let go of the need for others to ask for my forgiveness.

> ♥ *Heart Stretch*: *Close your eyes and relax your entire body beginning from the bottom of your feet all the way to the top of your head. Breathe in and out three times to keep your attention on your body. Now focus on your heart and rest your hand there. From this place, consider the following quote from my friend Amy Joy: "Understanding replaces forgiveness in the mind of the master."*
>
> - *What does this quote mean to you? How does this quote feel?*
> - *Is there anyone in your life, right now, whom you would like to forgive?*
> - *Is there anyone in your life, right now, whom you are struggling to forgive?*
> - *Have you forgiven yourself? How could you forgive yourself more?*

Making mistakes

To understand our lack of forgiveness at work, consider how we deal with mistakes, in our personal lives and in the workplace.

When my children were little, they'd often sing, "Mistakes are good, they help us grow, they teach us what we need to know." Over time however, they adopted a different attitude toward mistakes at school. Most grown-ups, too, have a hard time making mistakes at work. This is especially true for leaders. If a leader believes they should know everything, they can be unforgiving toward themselves and others. When I was a leader, though, I didn't have a problem with staff pointing out my mistakes. In fact, I loved surrounding myself with people who knew things I didn't. This attitude was possible only because I was okay with my own abilities and areas of growth. It's wonderful when staff are comfortable enough to talk about errors because it means we've created an atmosphere of safety and truth.

> ♥ *Heart Stretch*: *Close your eyes and relax your entire body beginning from the bottom of your feet all the way to the top of your head. Breathe in and out three times to keep your attention on your body. Now focus on your heart and rest your hand there. From this place, reflect on your relationship with mistakes:*
>
> - *How comfortable are you making mistakes?*
> - *How comfortable are you making mistakes in the workplace?*
> - *How do you feel about others who make mistakes? What if they do this often?*

A truly compassionate organization is one where compassion and love are practiced during the most challenging times—when things go awry. I'm not talking about dealing with a death or tragedy for one or many of the staff, although it's important to support one another during our most difficult personal experiences so we can feel valued, seen, and heard. I'm talking about having compassion and love when people don't act correctly or have performance issues.

In a conversation with Maya Angelou, bell hooks asked, "How do we hold people accountable for wrongdoing and yet at the same time remain in touch with their humanity enough to believe in their capacity to be transformed?"[1] We can treat others with compassion and love, even when their behavior is challenging. But listening to those who challenge us the most and engaging in dialogue with them always starts with the self. A compassionate and loving culture is made up of individuals who are practicing self-compassion and come together to support and reinforce policies and procedures that reflect their values.

Living in the energy of our values

I don't know any organization that doesn't list their organizational values. The most common organizational values tend to be loyalty, honesty, accountability, integrity, and value for money. Few companies have the words "love," "compassion," or "kindness" at the core of their business, although this is changing.[2] Regardless of the values stated, the test of whether a company acts on them comes at times of perceived crisis. Do their values hold steady in the face of cash-flow issues, layoffs, and other workplace woes? How do the values of loyalty, integrity, honesty, and transparency hold up? Are they loyal when a staff member makes a mistake, or does loyalty only go one way, from the worker to the business? Do they treat people with integrity during terminations? Are they honest and transparent about money issues, layoffs, cash-flow issues, or stakeholder bonuses?

Remember that the energy of the people in an organization determines whether the organization acts according to its stated values. If the energy of the workplace is one of fear, it will be challenging for staff to be compassionate even if leadership says compassion is one of their values. Compassion can occur only when our stress reactions are relaxed enough for us to get curious. If the energy of most of the staff is compassionate and loving, then that's how they'll react when challenges arise.

Staff and leadership who are living in the energy of the values live these values every day and with every person they meet. The values don't change depending on the circumstances. Leaders who embody their values, remind staff, when challenges arise, who they are. They don't allow external factors to dictate how they treat others.

> ♥ **Heart Stretch**: *Close your eyes and relax your entire body beginning from the bottom of your feet all the way to the top of your head. Breathe in and out three times to keep your attention on your body. Now focus on your heart and rest your hand there. From this place, think of your current workplace and answer these questions:*
>
> - *Do the staff or leadership embody the spirit of the company's values? Or is the energy as illustrated by their actions the opposite of the values the company says it espouses?*
> - *What may be preventing you or others from being in the energy of enacting your values?*

Difficult conversations

One reason workplaces have a hard time embodying their values is that people struggle to have difficult conversations at work. Difficult-conversation training seldom addresses the emotions we face when we talk about things that make us uncomfortable or dysregulate us. Often, this training doesn't teach us how to meet our own needs while leaning into the needs of others. Sometimes, we're uncomfortable saying things that validate our experience so we subdue our needs in order to belong. However, our sense of belonging begins and ends with us. When we belong to ourselves, nobody can tell us we don't belong. What others say or do does not change how we perceive ourselves. And the more authentic we are, the more attractive we are to those who appreciate who we are.

"Wherever you go, there you are" is one of my favorite quotes. At a simple level, it's true: where you are is where you find yourself physically. But when we look beyond the surface of this quote, it reveals something quite meaningful. No matter where we find ourselves geographically, our beliefs and emotions about ourselves or our lack of self-love are there with us. We could move to the end of the world, but until we change our energy or vibration, our experiences will be exactly the same. In fact, when people meet us, they meet our energy first. This is why people whose inner energy doesn't match their outer expression seem inauthentic or disingenuous. If we believe we're unlovable or unworthy or feel undervalued, we'll continue to have experiences that reinforce this view until we deal with this emotional baggage and give ourselves what we're seeking from others. This is why people who haven't dealt with their issues continue to meet the same person in a different body or have the same experiences with different people.

Sometimes we're aligned with work environments that make it challenging for us to address difficult feelings or have difficult conversations. These workplaces, which are often fear- or crisis-based, can also make it hard to acknowledge the humanity of other people. In the past, I was attracted to those workplaces because that's where I was emotionally. I was anxious, had a hard time relaxing, and constantly worried about my well-being. No wonder I gravitated toward workplaces with the same energy.

What does this have to do with difficult conversations? Well, the first difficult conversation we need to have is with ourselves. If we want to lean into the needs of others and get curious about them, we must also do these things for ourselves. We have to get honest about what we feel, what we need, and who we are. This takes courage. It's easier to blame someone else for our problems. But until we accept responsibility for our lives, nothing will change.

When we're not used to listening to ourselves and don't know what we need, taking responsibility for our lives takes practice. But when we understand what we're thinking and feeling each moment, we can give ourselves love and compassion. As we practice, we can also reach out to others for support, but if we don't know how we want them to support us, the interactions will be frustrating. I'm very good now at telling my husband when

I need him to listen to me vent versus when I'm coming to him for advice to solve a problem. I used to struggle with this. I'd go to him for support, expecting him to just listen to me, and would get frustrated when he tried to solve my problem. When I stopped expecting him to guess what I needed, my needs and expectations were met.

Often when we struggle with someone, it's because we have specific needs we feel aren't being met. When we fully understand what we need, we can ask for it from ourselves and other people. Alternatively, when we get better at meeting our own needs, we can get curious about other people's needs. We can ask them whether they need to vent or need a solution to a problem.

In my journey to enabling difficult but productive conversations, I also learned a powerful lesson. When I'm unsure about what to do, I pause—I do nothing until I have greater clarity. I shared this thought with my friend Debbie, who said, "In a world where we're taught to act, that's great advice."

Creating a work plan

One of the closest things we have to forgiveness at work is the work plan. For those who are not familiar, a workplan is something given to workers who are having issues performing at work. Work plans give staff the opportunity to change their behavior and improve their outcomes. I see work plans as an opportunity for course correction. The earlier they're implemented, the better. Once the boat is too far off course, it will take more and more work to steer it back on track.

There are many misconceptions about work plans. Sometimes, employees see them as preparation for termination. I would hope this isn't the case. If an organization invests time and money in an employee, the last thing it wants is to terminate them. If you're putting someone on a work plan only because you want to terminate them, then you're wasting everyone's time. Everyone deserves an opportunity to reflect and pivot, if they want to.

The most effective and compassionate work plans are those that help employees reflect on and understand their behavior in a more positive way: they are positive and compassionate mirrors of the person's experience. These work plans have the following characteristics:

The scenarios below are fictional. They are an amalgamation of real experiences I had over twenty years in the workplace. Any association to real life situations or people is purely coincidental.

- **They are supportive rather than punitive.** In my leadership positions, I've sometimes observed the desire to punish those who behave in ways we don't agree with. Punishment seems like a good deterrent. Except it's not. Performance issues occur when individuals need the most support. They signal that it's time to get curious about what's going on with our employees. For example, many people suffer in silence because of personal issues that impact how they perform at work. The larger the organization, the less we understand who people really are. How many of our colleagues are facing domestic violence issues at home? How many are facing poverty? How many are facing issues with caregiving for elderly parents? A compassionate approach may be to offer these people a temporary shift in position or paid leave to help them get through a challenging time.

- **They are truthful.** If I had a dime for every work plan I saw that wasn't clear and truthful I'd be rich. The most effective work plans are created with a staff member after a candid conversation about both side's worries. Employers can start the conversation by giving the person the benefit of the doubt and speaking only about observations rather than making assumptions. For example, we had an employee Burton who was absent 35 per cent of the time. We were able to show them on a calendar how many days they had been away. We learned in conversation that they were not in the right job. Even though they were not ready to admit it, their body was telling them every day that they dreaded going to work. I've also seen people suffer from chronic illness because they're not dealing with unaddressed emotions. A referral to a career coach could have gotten them on the right track.

- **They consider the whole being.** Another staff member, Dewey, was struggling with performance issues that negatively impacted his clients and team members. HR, acting from a place of curiosity, sat down with Dewey and asked him about his performance. Dewey had a lot of anxieties and was "known" around the office for being a complainer. Sometimes the people who complain the most are labeled disagreeable when what they really have is unmet needs. But Dewey's behavior was impacting the people he worked with, and his manager couldn't take it anymore.

First, we talked about how Dewey's behavior was impacting his teammates. But the larger conversation was about what was going on with Dewey, what was at the root of his anxiety. Together, we developed a plan to help manage his mental health, including flexibility and increased support from his manager. At the end of the work plan, Dewey's behavior had greatly improved, and he was feeling better overall.

- **They are equitable, not equal.** When I was in leadership and suggested an accommodation, I'd sometimes hear, "Well, if we do this for x, we'll have to do this for everybody." Many times, this fear had no basis in reality. When we start "what if-ing," we risk making gross generalizations about people's intentions. All staff, including leadership, want to be seen as human beings, and they want approaches tailored to their needs. When we think about approaching people who are suffering and behave poorly at work, we must consider how they want to be helped. If we go back to our definition of compassion, it must be given without judgment. It's possible that the help a worker desires, can't be offered by the organization. For example, workers may want paid leave to manage their affairs. If the company leadership can't offer it, that's fair. However, they should be honest about it and have HR support the person in achieving their goal in other ways. As leaders, this isn't the time to judge the person for desiring something that may not meet our needs; we shouldn't be afraid of them taking something from us since in, an infinite universe, endless possibilities exist.

One of the most effective ways that I found to shift myself from a place of fear to one of compassion was to ask myself, If this was me, how would I want to be treated? Please note that I didn't ask myself, What would I want? Sometimes we give people what we think they would want if they were us and then judge them based on how we would behave. All of us want to be treated with compassion, support, and care; we all want to participate and have a voice. Asking people what they need in the moment goes a long way in supporting them in the workplace.

Terminating someone with compassion

Terminations often feel challenging, which is why compassion on all sides is required. Sometimes terminations are inevitable despite everyone's best efforts; they're necessary to help workers and the organization on their journey. The termination itself isn't the issue; rather, it's the energy behind the termination. We can conduct a termination filled with fear, anger, and the desire to punish, or we can release the staff from a place of love and with good wishes. Terminations carried out in a spirit of well-wishing and compassion tend to be less acrimonious. I'd rather give people a generous package to make their exit more pleasant and wish them well than pay legal fees and still end up with a negative experience on all sides. Sometimes, terminating someone can be the most compassionate thing to do. People may be stuck in a job they don't like, held there by pay and benefits. We used to call this the "golden handcuffs." In these cases, a termination might be the push they need to start a new job, a new career, or a new business.

When I was in leadership, lawyers guided how we handled things. The way we communicated the termination to staff was constricted, and everyone signed a nondisclosure agreement. This is understandable, but the unintended consequence was that people simply disappeared. This approach not only frightens the staff that remains, it dishonors the time the person had with the organization, even if it was short.

One of the best things I learned from previous employers is to ask the person leaving the organization how they want their departure communicated. The person was an employee who deserves respect, regardless of what occurred with leadership. We want to treat them with honor and humanity because this is who we choose to be. We can choose to remember a person's worth regardless of what occurs. Communicating someone's departure with compassion also shows staff that we don't see them as one-dimensional characters; it helps us recognize that a person's departure will impact different people in different ways.

But what does terminating someone with compassion look like? It depends on the people involved. First, leadership must address its own needs and fears. When a termination occurs, it's because someone did something the company deemed unacceptable. Hopefully, the person was given plenty of support and opportunities to turn things around. Leadership or HR staff must then deal with their own negative perspectives and feelings about the person. Human beings have a tendency to judge others, so it's natural to feel angry, upset, or taken advantage of, but until we address those difficult feelings, we won't be able to treat the person in question with kindness. Thus, the first step is for those responsible for handling a termination to put on an oxygen mask so they can address their own discomfort with compassion. Once we meet our needs, we can lean into the conversation with the person facing termination, who will also be dealing with difficult feelings. We can make space for those feelings without accepting responsibility for them. What I mean is that the person being terminated may see themselves as a victim. They may not be able to tell themselves that they're responsible for their exit from the company. We can choose to lean into their difficult emotions and still treat them with care. We don't need to get triggered by them.

♥ *Heart Stretch*: *Close your eyes and relax your entire body beginning from the bottom of your feet all the way to the top of your head. Breathe in and out three times to keep your attention on your body. Now focus on your heart and rest your hand there. From this place, reflect on your experience with terminations:*

- *Think about a time you were terminated. How was it handled? Were you placed on a work plan? Did it have all the components mentioned above?*
- *Now think about a time when you had to terminate someone. Was it handled similarly? Or did you handle it differently? What challenging feelings come up for you when we discuss using compassion when terminating someone?*
- *If you were never terminated nor never had to terminate someone, think about a time when a difficult relationship had to come to an end. How did you manage this? Did the relationship end in a compassionate way or are there still unresolved feelings.*

Chapter 15

When Life Gives Us a Push

Be like a bamboo. It bends but does not break. It is flexible
yet deeply rooted.
~ Japanese proverb

I was lying in bed one night, staring at the ceiling. I knew I wanted to leave my workplace, but I was afraid. I was unhappy where I was and had a deep desire in my heart to do something different. My responsibilities at work were ramping up so now was the time to make a decision. I could either leave my workplace or stay in my current job and fully commit to being there. I could no longer sit on the fence of my ambivalence.

So as per my failsafe for when I ran out of options, I turned to God/Source/Universe. This was, of course, before I realized that Source/God/Universe doesn't exist outside of me. "If you want me to leave this workplace and do something else," I said petulantly to God/Source, "you've got to give me some runway, because I can't do both."

Two days later, it came in the most unexpected manner, in the form of a termination package. I was shocked. When I look back, however, I understand that this is the only way I would have left the security of my job. I'm so deeply grateful for that experience. Since then, I've received a number of opportunities that have allowed me to continue on this path of following my passions. Every seemingly negative event contains within it the gift of opportunity and the seeds of our dreams.

Transforming seeming negatives into positives

David used to be fascinated by alchemy. He'd speak to me about the ability to transform challenging situations into incredible gifts. Traditionally, alchemy means transforming one base medal into another metal—usually alchemizing iron or aluminum into something more valuable like silver or gold. Alchemy is often viewed as magical and mystical. Although there is no evidence that physical alchemy exists, this book invites you to transform all your challenges at work and in your life into pure gold.

When I think back to the early days of writing this book, I realize that instead of staying in the energy of my fear, I alchemized the challenge of not having income and not being busy into an opportunity to write. I also took a short-term position at a university to teach about doing research. The experience was enriching, and I met some incredible young people with whom I was able to share self-love and self-compassion practices. I alchemized my difficult moment by asking myself positive "what if" questions. What if this is the best thing that ever happened to me? What if I never worried about money, or anything else for that matter? These positive questions allowed me to get into the energy of receiving.

In my journey to greater mastery, I no longer give as much power to what's happening externally. When challenges come up, I go inward to understand my own alignment. When life feels the most challenging, it's also ripe with opportunities for positive change. During challenging moments, I use the negative emotions that come up to reaffirm who I want to be and what I want to experience. I say, "Thank you for the opportunity to reaffirm who I choose to be."

This book is an invitation to master ourselves and, by transforming ourselves, to transform the world around us, including how we work. We have to work harder on ourselves than we do at our job! By viewing the most difficult challenges at work and in our lives as gifts, and by realigning them to our ideal state, we can shift our perspectives from that of victim to master. By leaning into difficult moments with the full support and presence of ourselves and others, we can alchemize racism, bullying, and harassment; toxic work environments; "power over" approaches; and other relationship problems into opportunities for growth, healing, and love. True alchemy requires persistence, courage, faith, and, most importantly, love. Love and compassion for ourselves and others keep us in the game when we want to give up. In our most challenging moments, we must use the elixirs of love and compassion to regenerate ourselves so we can move toward fulfilling our dreams.

♥ **Heart Stretch**: *Close your eyes and relax your entire body beginning from the bottom of your feet all the way to the top of your head. Breathe in and out three times to keep your attention on your body. Now focus on your heart and rest your hand there. From this place, do the following:*

- *Imagine you're an alchemist who can convert challenging experiences into gold. You're wearing a magic hat in a room full of potions and elixirs.*
- *There's a cauldron in front of you. Pour your challenge into the cauldron. Reflect on what you would want to experience instead of what's in the cauldron. For example, if you're in a toxic work environment and want to experience one with more love, add more love to the cauldron.*
- *When you're done transforming your experience into a potion, drink it. Allow yourself to feel the alchemy now that you're in a more compassionate workplace.*

This exercise will reveal two things. The first is how good your imagination is—a good imagination is the key to embodying a new identity. The second is how open you are to experiences outside your comfort zone. Sometimes, we're not comfortable with play. If this is you, ask your inner guide, What will help you move forward?

Reframing failure

While most of us are discouraged by our failures, successful entrepreneurs embrace failure as a potential opportunity. They're often not hampered by setbacks; rather, they see them for the gifts they are. I once heard someone say that truly successful people never ask themselves, Can I do this? They instead ask, How can I do this? In their minds, there's no doubt they can accomplish their dream. It's solely a matter of how the dream will come about.

If we remove the judgment from the perceived failure, all that's left is experience. We're constantly having experiences that tell us who we're being in every moment. Experiences give us information about what we want and don't want. Personally, I knew my failures were a gift. They were guiding me toward who I wanted to be or what I wanted to do. Now, when I face failure, I think it's either not the right thing or not the right time, and then I go inward to figure out which one it is.

I love sharing the story of Jack Ma, billionaire co-owner of Alibaba. He got rejected from thirty jobs and from Harvard ten times! He's now worth $24 billion. I believe he faced all those rejections because he wasn't meant to take any of those paths. If he had, he probably wouldn't have founded Alibaba. From my perspective, had he gone inward, perhaps he could have saved himself all that work! But maybe not. He undoubtedly learned something from the experiences.

To alchemize failure, we must understand that failure isn't failure at all. More important, we must see that what we perceive as failure doesn't say anything about us. It doesn't mean we're not worthy or loveable or that we can't achieve our dreams. Once we understand some of our core beliefs about failure, we can choose what we want to embody. This sounds easy, but alchemizing our thoughts is like planting a garden. It takes effort and patience. It takes trust that the seeds we plant will sprout, even when nothing happens at first. To keep our garden growing, we need to focus on the seeds that sprouted, not the ones that didn't work out.

> ♥ *Heart Stretch*: *Close your eyes and relax your entire body beginning from the bottom of your feet all the way to the top of your head. Breathe in and out three times to keep your attention on your body. Now focus on your heart and rest your hand there. From this place, reflect on your relationship with failure:*
>
> - *Think about the times you might have "failed" in your life. What were those experiences like? How did you feel when you failed?*
> - *Do you treat yourself with compassion when you fail, or do you treat yourself with criticism and anger?*
> - *What are some of the core beliefs that underlie your relationship with failure?*
> - *What would help you shift your perspective on failure?*

Receiving a work plan

Receiving a work plan can be frightening! Our thoughts tend to go to the worst-case scenario. Will I lose my job? Will I lose my house? What will happen to me? Am I not good enough? It is absolutely okay to have complex feelings about receiving a work plan. Don't resist these feelings.

A work plan is a true opportunity for self-evaluation. Sometimes it takes a wake-up call to make us realize we're heading where we don't want to go. I've found that the Universe/Source/God will help us along the way if we listen to the messages all around us. If we don't listen, the messages get louder and louder. They can come via workplace issues or life events such as an illness. These messengers are helpers; they are course corrections for our lives.

An employee facing or on a work plan can see it as an opportunity to ask questions:

- Am I in the right job?
- Do I love what I'm doing, or am I just here for the paycheck?
- What else is going on in my life that could be impacting my performance at work?
- What is this experience telling me?
- How can I turn this situation into the best thing that has ever happened to me? How can I alchemize this challenging situation into an opportunity to live my dream?

When we open ourselves to the potential that exists in every moment, not just negative possibilities, we're more likely to see endless opportunities all around us.

Chapter 16

Addressing Toxicity
with Compassion

When the roots are deep,
there is no reason to fear the wind.
~ Unknown

"I guess I can see it from both sides," David chimed in as I was talking to our daughter about having compassion and love in race and equity work. "From a spiritual perspective, we're all Source. AND from a human perspective, there are groups of individuals who are being killed and hurt by another group or groups. So, one does not negate the other. We can't deny the experience of living here on earth."

This is what David calls "living from the AND." When you live from the AND, your perspective shifts from separation to interconnectedness. The AND, as he calls it, invites us to move from dualistic us-and-them thinking to the concept of greater unity. Living from the AND helps us understand differing perspectives without the need for labeling them as right or wrong. His comments resonated because this has been my experience. My white friends seemed desperate to know how to support marginalized people, but they didn't know how to manage internal conflict between what they had been taught and what they were being told. My white friends also didn't know how to support themselves through their feelings of shame and guilt. My nonwhite friends wanted to be acknowledged—to be seen, heard, and valued—and they were tired of trying to make white people understand their needs. My friends also had a genuine fear for their personal safety.

Because we haven't learned how to properly manage these difficult emotions, we've created a society where there's a lot of reactivity and not a lot of listening, leaning in, and loving. As we talk about these difficult emotions in this chapter, hold onto the vision of living in the AND.

Making judgments

Before we discuss making judgments, it's important to remember that judgments are different from observations. Observations are made without emotion. They describe what we believe we're observing in the moment. "He is wearing a red shirt" is an observation. Judgments, on the other hand, are subjective— opinions and conclusions about what we're observing. They usually reveal what we think should be or what we think should happen. For example, "He's a jerk" is a judgment. Sometimes we believe we're making an observation when we're in fact making a judgment. "The weather is good" is a judgment not an observation. Weather is neither good nor bad. But we could say, "It's sunny"—that's an observation.

Because we confuse observations with judgments, we tend to judge one another often. Right now, we live in a society where people are canceling one another because of judgments. Canceling occurs when the masses (or social media judges) decide that something a person might have said or done, at any point in their life, is unfavorable or unacceptable culturally and write that person off. This isn't surprising to me. For far too long we've silenced the victims; now we're silencing those we see as oppressors. But all canceling does is help us avoid uncomfortable feelings and difficult conversations, which we need to move society's relationships forward. From my perspective, we need to find a balance, one that silences no one, one that's open to all perspectives and allows us to lean into one another for discussion and healing. Of course, to accomplish this, we have to be aware of how we handle toxic behaviors. See Chapter 14 for greater insight.

When I was working in one organization, I heard a story about someone accused of making racist remarks to someone else. The person sharing the story was clearly outraged. Historically, we haven't believed victims' stories about violence, bullying, and harassment, especially female victims. Now we tend to validate people's experiences. But the flip side is that people are sometimes accused and judged before all the information is provided. I hate to admit it, but I've been caught in situations where I later found out that my judgment wasn't perceived as impartial. I'd never purposely accuse someone of consciously harming another without evidence, but subconsciously I might have already made up my mind.

This was a hard pill to swallow. But it was an invaluable lesson. Often, we don't realize we're judging others or biased. We may subconsciously side with the victim or the accuser. In these situations, I recommend that organizations bring in outside people to deal with it. However, even then, I'm not sure we can ever be fully unbiased, as individual perceptions shape our experience.

> ♥ *Heart Stretch: Close your eyes and relax your entire body beginning from the bottom of your feet all the way to the top of your head. Breathe in and out three times to keep your attention on your body. Now focus on your heart and rest your hand there. From this place, reflect on your relationship with judgments. For example, I once did a thought experiment to see how long I could go without making a judgment. I promised myself I'd put ten cents in a jar every time I had a judging thought. Oh man. I didn't get through half a day without putting a lot of dimes in the jar.*
>
> - *What has been your experience with judgments? Have you ever judged someone and been wrong? Has someone ever wrongly judged you?*
> - *How do you feel about the current cancel culture?*
> - *Based on what you've learned about curiosity, what role does compassion play in decreasing judgment?*

Reimagining how we deal with bullying

We've all heard the saying "hurt people hurt people." But this is too simplistic an explanation of bullying. Not everyone who was hurt becomes a person who hurts others. However, people who have been hurt *and* who perceive themselves as victims are more likely to hurt others, or themselves. As we continue to study trauma, we're developing a better understanding of how our histories and the stories we tell ourselves about who we are and who others are shape how we perceive and interact with them. I see trauma-informed practice as the stepping stone to compassion because it helps us understand people's behavior from the perspective of someone whose survival strategies are no longer working. These survival strategies may have helped them avoid further abuse or getting hurt, but under different contexts they are dysfunctional and hurtful. Trauma-informed practice builds greater understanding of why people behave the way that they do. It allows us to have greater love, compassion, and kindness and, eventually, to forgive.

Note that I don't use the word "pity." Pity isn't the same as compassion or empathy. In fact, pity is a disempowering emotion. When we pity someone, energetically, we feel we're above them: we don't see them as the capable, powerful beings they truly are. Pity causes us to disengage.

So what can we do when someone is bullying another person? The "no tolerance" approach placates rather than problem solves. In fact, when we treat bullying with harshness, it only reinforces the bully's perception that they are a victim, so their perspective doesn't change.

But what if we treated bullying a different way? If bullies see themselves as victims, helping them find compassion and love for themselves might help them understand how their behavior has impacted others. Now some might say, "Well, aren't we rewarding that behavior?" I can assure you we're not. Bullies have a harsh inner voice, which can make it challenging to find love and compassion for themselves, especially when addressing the shame and guilt of facing termination or a work plan.

Additionally, because being a victim and a perpetrator are, energetically, two sides of the same coin, both parties can use compassion work to support themselves. I'd love to see workplaces offer compassion-based training to both sides. Please note that when I say these two roles are aligned, I'm not saying that anything is the victim's fault. Even if we align with a negative experience, we don't consciously choose to hurt ourselves. Often these alignments come from unhealed hurts. It is, however, our responsibility to heal ourselves and to no longer give our power away to other people. By staying angry at the person who is bullying, we're keeping ourselves at the same vibrational level. When we get stuck in victim mode, we fail to see and understand how truly powerful we are.

♥ *Heart Stretch*: *Close your eyes and relax your entire body beginning from the bottom of your feet all the way to the top of your head. Breathe in and out three times to keep your attention on your body. Place your hand on your heart and direct your focus there. Think about your experiences with bullying. Recall a time when you were bullied or you bullied someone. For each type of experience, ask yourself these questions:*

- *What am I feeling right now? What is going on for me? Now offer yourself some reassuring words such as "This is hard" or "This hurts."*

- *What does my heart need in this moment? Note that it's important to ask your heart not your mind because your mind will project it out. For example, if you're feeling sad, your mind may say, "I need Joe to stop being such a jerk" instead of "I need reassurance because I feel sad." When your heart tells you what it needs, offer it an affirmation such as "May I be happy," "May I feel safe," "I am happy," or "I am safe." Repeat the affirmation until the stress drains away and you relax. Now from this place of calm, reflect on the following.*

- *What was going on with the person who was bullying me? If you're unprepared to think about this, don't worry. Try another day when you can.*

- *What was going on with me that caused me to hurt someone? What did I believe that enabled me to act this way? Be compassionate with yourself.*

- *What must it have been like to be hurt by me? What could or can I do to repair or restore the relationship?*

This reflection may feel really challenging. During the most difficult moments, allow yourself to get some space between yourself and your emotions. For example, focus on the noises outside, or something you feel like your feet on the floor. When you are ready to release the reflection, focus on your breath as a way to give yourself compassion. Breathe in and out three times saying, "I breathe in love for myself, and breathe our love for others."

Victims or oppressors?

Addressing racism and other "isms' can feel so uncomfortable that we might avoid it out of fear of making a mistake. But denying the existence of these "isms" doesn't make them disappear. It only further contributes to the problem.

We may resist dealing with racism because we think we have no power over the situation. To create a world with greater equality, love, and compassion, we must have courage. We need courage to discuss issues that bring us to the edge of our comfort zone. It's the only way to get closer to one another so we can end the divisions that currently exist in our world.

If we're going to discuss racism, we have to go back to the colonizers. It's paradoxical that colonizers were deemed the "fittest" in the so-called survival game. In fact, the survival-of- the-fittest argument has, for far too long been used to justify the use of violence in the same way the compassion rhetoric is sometimes hijacked. How can people so afraid of not having enough that they murder and take advantage of other people be considered powerful? Unconditional love and compassion are the hardest and most challenging approaches in the face of fear. To be able to look at ourselves and see all the terrible things we've aligned ourselves with, or that we've allowed into our world, and still be able to forgive and love ourselves and others takes enormous courage. We need extraordinary strength to not hate, to not bow down to our own anger and our need for punishment. We need to be brave to not lose who we truly are in the illusion of separation.

It's interesting to me that white supremacists often use the rhetoric of victimhood in their desire to protect their own kind. They say they feel vulnerable to nonwhites and worry about their rights being taken away. But to nonwhites, they seem powerful. White supremacists feel at the affect of nonwhite folks, which is why their efforts are about increasing white power. If they saw themselves as powerful, they wouldn't need more power at the expense of other groups. As our friend Tony McAleer says in Chapter 7, those who are practicing hate need to find their own power from within rather than attempting to take it from other people. They need to find compassion and love for their own experiences and address their own traumas to avoid spilling them onto others.

Why do white supremacists feel this way? Perhaps they see people of color and Indigenous peoples as powerful. More and more stories are being told about the powerful ways that Indigenous and Black people have used to overcome their history. In fact, even after experiencing genocide, our Indigenous brothers and sisters have reclaimed the power that was always within them as evidenced in the Canadian Idle No More movement and the Truth and Reconciliation Commission. I'm in awe of how, despite losing their identity and their children, Indigenous peoples have continued to stand up for their rights and continue to work for improved treatment in Canada. Similarly, the Black Lives Matter movement is an approach to bring greater awareness to the overt and sometimes covert racism that our brothers and sisters experience. We can't decide who we're going to choose to be, if we're not aware of what we have been. Right now, our world is a giant mirror demonstrating to us who we are.

Dealing with racism with compassion

But how do we address issues of racism in a way that brings us closer together rather than tears us apart? First, we have to admit that we've all contributed to the problem. Yes ... *all of us,* through acts of omission or commission. If we're experiencing it or witnessing it, we're contributing to it. Our level of consciousness has contributed to the world we've created. Remember that in our individual lives, we've separated ourselves from who we truly are and from our fellow human beings. We contribute to racism and other "isms" every time we treat others as different or as separate from us. When we exclude others and view ourselves as different, whether for better or worse, we're automatically creating the conditions that enable racism, sexism, classism to exist, because all of these "isms" are about othering. When we don't care about what's happening to other people because we don't see it as our problem, we're othering people. Conversely, we're interconnected, so what we do for others, we do for ourselves. I've excluded others out of fear of them hurting me or hurting someone I care about; therefore, in micro ways, I, too, have contributed to racism. In the past, I've also remained silent when overhearing comments of a racist nature for fear of being excluded or making a scene.

One of the worst examples of separating ourselves from others, outside of slavery, is the Holocaust. This horrific treatment of Jewish people is often attributed to one man, Hitler. However, remember my comment about the value of the first and subsequent followers? If people hadn't followed Hitler, he would have remained a lone nut. Why did 10 million of our brothers and sisters follow him? The mere existence of a world war illustrates just how far removed we were, as human beings, from our true nature.

Historically, attempts to introduce greater compassion and love have been extinguished by us as soon as they showed promise, as illustrated by the death of Dr. Martin Luther King Jr. On April 5, 1968, the day after his assassination, his dear friend Thich Nhat Hanh wrote, "They killed Martin Luther King. They killed us. I am afraid the root of violence is so deep in the heart and mind and manner of this society. They killed him. They killed my hope. I do not know what to say. This country was able to produce King, but cannot preserve King."[1] Dr. King was one of the few people in this world who fully supported the energy of love as the solution to all our problems. He understood that reacting to hate in an angry, oppositional way only fans the flames.

One of the most profound sayings I've heard comes from Kahuna Nui Hale Kealohalani Makua, who said, "Love all you see, with humility."[2] But what does it mean to "love all"? Does it mean to love your enemies? Does it mean to love all the negative things in your life? Does it mean to love all that causes you pain and fear? This saying challenges me to remember that if everything comes from Source/God/Universe, then everything is good, or for my good, even the seemingly negative. I believe this relates to David's discussion of allowing all things to be. If we understand that we created these things, then, through love, we can shift out of them. In fact, whenever I've transmuted the energy of fear into love, I've experienced the gift in the moment. It hasn't always felt comfortable to make that choice, but love has an amazing way of realigning us with the highest level of vibration possible. Additionally, when I examine my life, most of the time I see that I've been my biggest enemy. It's only when I've turned into my best friend that my life has turned around.

> ♥ **Heart Stretch**: *Close your eyes and relax your entire body beginning from the bottom of your feet all the way to the top of your head. Breathe in and out three times to keep your attention on your body. Now focus on your heart and rest your hand there. From this place, answer these questions:*
>
> - *Are you your own best friend or your own worst enemy?*
> - *What if our greatest enemies are actually our greatest friends in that they're forcing us to truly stand in our own self-love, personal power, and authority?*
> - *How can we turn the energy we use to create racism into something that could benefit us all?*

To effectively address issues of race and equity, we must put our oxygen masks and take care of our inherent needs. Only then can we be open to the perspective of others. Remember, too, that the perspectives of others—no matter how prejudiced, hurtful, or detrimental they may appear—need not have power over us. They need not hurt us. I've heard many of my nonwhite friends say, "Hey, it's not my job to educate white people on privilege." They're correct.

People who identify as racialized need to tend to their own needs and allow others to do the work of leaning in. Some, however, like me, who have benefited from being white passing, are willing to talk about race to understand what truly motivates it or, rather, what people who seek to oppress others really need.

There will always be times when we're triggered by another person, especially in challenging conversations around race. In these moments, it's important to lean out, to tend to our own needs, and then lean back in and get curious again. I recommend that the other person also do this, after they've worked through their own shame, guilt, trauma, and so on. Each person is responsible for giving themselves what they need to stay engaged and open to change and growth in every moment.

Race and equity issues, whether in the workplace or not, are best managed in an energy of humility and curiosity and from a true desire to understand, support, and repair. Restorative justice is a compassionate approach; it's not so much about punishing as it is about closure and coming together. I don't think people always realize how challenging it is to face someone we've hurt and ask them for forgiveness and what we can do to repair the relationship. It's easier to be punished by an external person and to see ourselves as the victim. In the end, the relationship has to take precedence over being right. And the results will be what we desire, since when we truly care about each other, we try not to hurt each other. Even if we make a mistake—for example, in the terms or pronouns we use—then focusing on the energy of love and forgiveness will help us ask for forgiveness from others and will help us be supportive of one another.

It isn't surprising to me that people react in a negative manner when issues of gender identity or race come up. People who get upset about gender-inclusive language and using proper pronouns are acting out of fear. They fear they're going to lose something if they make a mistake or if there are expectations they're unable to meet. They're still energized by feelings of victimhood; they believe others have power over them. Once they acknowledge those fears and release them, they'll see that there's nothing to fear in offering to others what they say they need from us. Nobody can take from us more than we're willing to give. It would be helpful if workplaces had compassion-based training on gender inclusivity that focused on people's discomfort around gender pronouns. Mandatory training and punitive approaches often result in greater resistance and opposition.

An extraordinary example of leaning in

I love sharing the story of Daryl Davis, a black jazz musician who had the courage to get curious about members of the KKK and ask them, "Why do you hate me, when you don't even know me?"[3] His story is told in the book *Klandestine Relationships*. But before sharing more of his story, I want to make the following proviso. First, I'm in no way saying that anyone should do what Mr. Davis did. It's important for us to listen to our own guidance regarding how to lean in, and to support ourselves through difficult conversations. Mr. Davis must have felt safe enough, though, to sit across from KKK members and talk to them about racism. He also attended KKK rallies and spoke to high-ranking members to understand the messaging being shared. I can only imagine the extraordinary courage Mr. Davis possessed and the faith he must have had, in himself and the people he spoke to. By offering white supremacists respect and nonjudgment, he got over three hundred KKK members to leave the clan.

This story is interesting because it's so uncommon. But it's an example of true alchemy. You see, Mr. Davis didn't seek to change white supremacists. He sought to understand them, and in that understanding, he created the circumstances that enabled those Klan members to change themselves. I believe he was able to sit with white supremacists because he could offer himself respect and kindness during those difficult conversations, particularly during disrespectful and demeaning dialogues. He didn't believe what they said about him was true; if he did, he wouldn't have been able to make a space for the dialogue. He didn't debate whether they deserved respect. He gave them what he wanted in return.

> ♥ **Heart Stretch**: *Close your eyes and relax your entire body beginning from the bottom of your feet all the way to the top of your head. Breathe in and out three times to keep your attention on your body. Now focus on your heart and rest your hand there. From this place, reflect on Daryl Davis's approach to compassion.*
>
> - *What other extraordinary stories of leaning in have you heard or experienced?*
> - *What would help you lean into difficult conversations?*

Chapter 17

Opening Up to Magic

The world is full of magical things,
patiently waiting for our sense to grow sharper.
~ W.B. Yeats

In statistics class, I learned that everything that falls outside the normal distribution isn't normal. Within the curve was the desirable place to be. It's not surprising that most of us love to live in the middle. The need to belong is so ingrained within us. In fact, most medications, clothing, furniture, and so on are made for those in the middle, or what we call the norm.

However, what lies outside the middle is extraordinary. Magic resides outside the curve. Abundance beyond compare, perfect health, true freedom, and living to be over a hundred are all beyond the curve, as is everything we desire right now. Reimagining work is about getting out of our normal structures to see past what we've decided is acceptable. For those of us who believe we can create a world where love and compassion are our default setting—our belief is outside the norm as well.

For me to be willing to live an extraordinary life, I had to step outside of the curve to question my alignments. It didn't always feel good, but it always turned out.

Deserving my magical life

Life is truly magical if we allow it to be. We deserve to live lives filled with magic, but not everyone believes this or thinks they deserve it. I like to use Louise Hays' affirmation, "I deserve the best life has to offer and I accept only the best now."[1] It helps me feel expansive; it helps me expect more, rather than settling for a mediocre life because that's what I think I deserve or can get. Letting go of the need to know how things will turn out or whether my dreams will come true has had an unexpected result. When I started believing I deserved more out of life, I received more out of life.

I remember contemplating turning my backyard into an extraordinary garden to share food with the community. I imagined beautiful sunflowers surrounding raised beds, but I hadn't done anything. I'd spent most of the spring sitting in the bliss of imagining it done.

In the fall, my husband pointed to a large weed-like stick. "Look. A sunflower's coming up."

"Really?" Yup. There it was. A sunflower. Nobody had planted it. For twelve years that spot had held nothing but grass. Now you might be thinking that I live in the country and that maybe some seeds flew in from other places. Perhaps. But in the twelve years I lived there, that never happened. Not until I contemplated sunflowers.

Sunflowers represent faith in God/Source/Universe, and they're special because they're always trying to find the light, just like us. This is why the cover of this book has a sunflower on it.

As I mentioned in Chapter 11, asking the question, Where is our power? can help us find our light during our darkest moments.

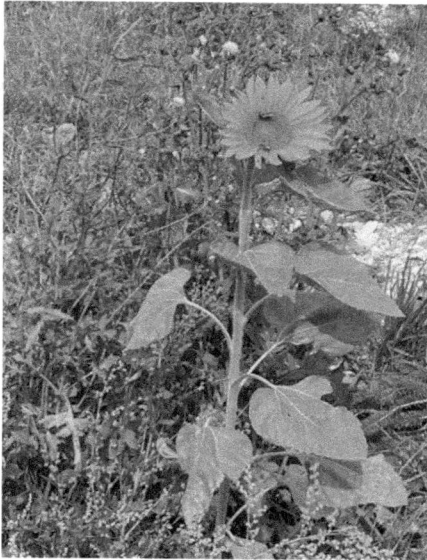

Figure 3. A sunflower that grew after
I imagined a field of sunflowers

This sunflower reminds me that I don't have to limit my dreams. And neither do you. The Universe/Source/God within us has magical ways to make our dreams come true, no matter how big or bold they may seem. We just have to believe they can happen and be in the mode of receivership. If we want to work, we can work, and if we don't want to work, we don't have to work. I've found that living from my passions is empowering. It doesn't feel like work at all. In our hearts lie our greatest desires. We just have to quiet our minds to truly hear them.

You have to be out of your mind.

"I must be out of my mind," I'd sometimes say to myself. Here I was, a new business owner who'd decided to listen to her inner voice rather than keep grinding it out. I was committed, but sometimes that inner voice would tell me to do something I felt was counterintuitive to achieving success. In that moment, I needed to go inward to face my fears or address my emotional baggage. There were days I spent primarily in meditation, cleaning up my energy. "Shouldn't I be doing something toward the business?" I'd ask my inner voice. Spending all day on my interior life felt antithetical to everything I'd been taught about success.

When doubt crept in and I couldn't support myself, I'd turn for support to my husband.

"You have to be out of the rational mind," he'd say.

He was mirroring what my inner voice was telling me, but he didn't realize that.

"The rational mind will always talk you out of your desires and tell you the worst-case scenario. You have to get beyond it," he said.

"Well, I sometimes feel like I'm out of my mind," I said.

I decided to fully trust my heart and let go. In the past, my mind always told me the most negative things possible. To move forward with my vision, I had to stop believing everything negative that it told me; I had to move beyond what I thought should happen and focus on getting my power back. My mind was like a risk adviser who instead of playing a supporting role in the company became its leader and saw everything as a risk. But the comfort zone is never the growth zone.

Sometimes my heart or inner voice told me something that seemed counter to what society dictates people should do in my situation.

"Allowing is the key. You have to allow the good into your life," David said.

Allowing helped me accept things that didn't make sense in my head but were the wishes of my heart. But allowing and not listening to my mind took time and persistence. There were times when my mind was too loud and when the thoughts were followed by fear-based emotions that wouldn't subside. When I couldn't soothe my mind, I'd soothe my body instead by practicing yoga, or Qigong or by moving the energy around via walking. Soothing my body helped me deal with the negative emotions so I could open up a space to think and feel differently.

A lot of this work is about self-soothing. Loving ourselves is about soothing ourselves in regard to everything that scares us. If we weren't soothed as children, we may be afraid of uncertainty or the unknown. But that's where the magic is. We self-soothe by offering ourselves words of kindness, love, and reassurance, by reminding ourselves that we have the power to overcome anything we experience. This takes courage. There have been times when I've been pushed to the edge, sitting on my mat, tears streaming down my face, feeling that I couldn't keep going, but I did. And it always worked out. I can always get myself back on track.

I'm now careful with my energy. Not in a way that reinforces a feeling of victimhood. Instead, I'm choosey about where I place my attention. I don't really like to listen to the news or to negative stories, especially about people, because I know that my thoughts will align with that negative energy.

Another technique that helps me give less weight to my negative thoughts is remembering all the incredible spiritual and hard-to-explain things I've experienced. I also rely on what my heart has to say on the matter. It always steers me in the right direction.

The heart always knows.

When I'm stuck between what my mind thinks and what my heart knows, I always choose my heart. But that wasn't always the case. There was a time when I didn't trust my heart because my mind told me that what the heart felt was wrong, or bad for me. Sometimes, the mind tells us not to trust our heart. Do we feel we fell in love with the wrong person because they were abusive? Or loved our parents even though they might have been hurtful? When the mind judges something as right or wrong, we start to mistrust everything around us, including ourselves.

When I started out on my entrepreneurial journey, everyone had an opinion about what I should do to succeed. I was told that if I followed this or that program or process, success would be inevitable.

Ignoring what my heart was telling me, I did it all: I paid for marketing, went on referral sites, focused on social media, and so on. It was exhausting, and to be honest, it didn't result in the opportunities I thought it would. I've since learned that there's no right way to make our dreams come true. The heart is a compass, directing us toward our dreams. And my heart was always correct, even if I didn't understand why it felt a particular way.

But how do we know it's our heart and not our mind speaking to us? That's a tough question to answer. The mind is tricky. Sometimes it feels like the heart is telling us to do something when it's really the mind. When I'm unsure, I do nothing until I receive further guidance. I usually speak to my heart by focusing on it and asking it what I want to know. The answers are usually not fear-based and feel expansive when I think about them. Also, when the answers are unexpected (not something I thought about), I'm certain my heart answered.

If you're not used to listening to your heart, or if it doesn't feel safe to do so, that's all right. We can meet ourselves where we are. I find when I focus on relaxing my body through exercise, Qigong, or yoga, my mind relaxes. When my body relaxes, I have more power over my mind, and this gives my heart an opportunity to feel safe enough to start talking again.

Aligning with our desires

Do you know how important you are? You probably don't. If you did, you wouldn't be reading this book. You are magnificent. You are beyond powerful. I believe every single being on this earth is an incredible, unique, and powerful aspect of God consciousness. I don't claim to know where we came from, but the fact that we even exist is a miracle. I believe Consciousness/God/Source created us to experience itself through us. So it makes sense that the Source within us wants us to live the most magnificent lives we can imagine. Negative emotions constrict us and prevent us from creating and expanding. All the metaphysical books I've read over my lifetime point to this conclusion.

I'm a long-time student of Neville Goddard, a metaphysics teacher on the power of thought and feeling. One of my favorite of his teachings is that every desire contains within it the seed of its realization. In other words, if a desire exists, it's a desire in the mind of God/Source, and its presence is already manifest and waiting to be experienced. Each seed has within it everything it needs to become a tree. Our desires contain everything they need to come to fruition. Our role is to allow these desires to be fulfilled. If we have a desire, it's because we've been chosen by that desire to be the source of its realization.

One of the key aspects of aligning with our desires is allowing the energy of our wishes to resonate within us. This means embodying the identity of the person whose desire has already occurred. Remember our pyramid? The more our emotions align with our desires, the more likely and faster they will appear in our physical reality. But doubts and worries, which cause us to feel fear, often ruin our ability to align with our desires. We spend too much time waiting for a desire to appear in the real world and get discouraged when we don't see it. The good news is this: if our emotions—for example, relief, gratitude, or happiness—are connected with our dreams coming true *most of the time,* then the desires will appear in our reality.

As I said earlier, most of us don't realize we're constantly creating our reality, we just do it subconsciously. If we create a reality we didn't desire, we don't need to get angry at ourselves, because we didn't do it on purpose. In my case, when a problem came up, I'd obsess about it. I'd focus on the worst-case scenario and dwell on how I'd respond if my desire didn't come true. I didn't realize I was negating my dream and creating within myself conflicting emotions.

By contrast, when I let go of my need to worry and believed that everything would work out positively, for the good of everyone, it always did. One strategy that helped me let go was to ask myself: If I accomplished my desire, what would I think of or do next? Reflecting on this question helped me stay positive.

Of course, there were times when I couldn't get out of my funk. If that happened, I sat with those emotions, gave them love, revised them at night when I was least resistant, and started over the next day.

Thinking about my sunflower, I believe our job is to feed our desires the same way we would a lovely garden. I plant my seeds in the fertile ground of optimism and joy. I feed my desires sunshine in the form of the belief that they will become a reality, and I water them with my faith and courage. I diligently pull out the weeds of negative thinking, fear, doubt, and worry, which prevent my desires from growing into fruition. One of my favorite ways to avoid getting discouraged when reality doesn't align with my desires is to tell myself that today's reality is yesterday's energy. Physical reality is the manifestation of your previous thoughts and beliefs and, most importantly, emotions. I became keenly aware of this when I started monitoring my thoughts and feelings.

If I'm putting all my focus on positive thoughts and beliefs, does this mean I'm practicing what some call "toxic positivity"? Does it mean I'm ignoring the bad? Absolutely not. First, I recommend paying attention to every emotion, whether it make sense in your mind or not. When we ignore emotions, they grow in intensity to get our attention. I welcome all my emotions with equal love and acceptance. I listen to them with as much presence as possible. They give me powerful messages about who I'm being in the moment. Besides, "toxic positivity" is a misnomer since nothing positive—such as love, compassion, or peace—can be truly toxic. What's toxic is attempting to make negative emotions wrong and deluding ourselves into thinking that we're not where we are. Resistance to feeling those difficult emotions is toxic to our bodies and minds. To shift out of this type of thinking, we have to look at what we've created more globally and then make a choice about who we're going to be in the next moment.

Why it's important to live our dreams

Think of the person you most admire or want to emulate. Is it Oprah or Warren Buffet or Jesus? There is absolutely no difference between you and that person. We are all created by the same Source/God. The difference between successful people and nonsuccessful people is that most people give up on their dreams when it gets tough. Others don't even begin to live their dreams because they talk themselves out of it.

But living our dreams is the key to creating a world where love and compassion reign. In fact, we owe it to one another to be abundant, joyful, happy, fulfilled, and healthy. It matters if we're flourishing because we're all interconnected. When people are in survival mode, they can't care about other people. They're too busy surviving. When we're feeling some sort of lack, we see others as the enemy, as competition, or as a threat. But when we feel fulfilled, we become aware of the abundance around us and how we're fully supported by the Universe/Godself. We understand that others are on their own journeys and that their journeys won't have any impact on us being able to fulfill our dreams. We start to enjoy witnessing the journeys of others. We love bearing witness to them.

While I was on a meditative retreat, my inner voice said to me, unexpectedly, "Each of us has a pot of gold, available at any point. Whether you tap into yours has nothing to do with others. Others cannot access what rightfully belongs to you." Whether we access this unending abundance depends on whether we have limiting beliefs. Knowing that abundance is everywhere helped me let go of my competitive nature; it allowed me to identify limiting beliefs regarding my own prosperity.

Additionally, because we're impacted by the behavior of others, it's important to live our dreams. The Wright Brothers fulfilled their dream of flying. And in fulfilling their dreams, they changed the way human beings travel forever. They opened up our borders, which allowed us to expand our connection to others. Right now, whatever our dreams are, there will be people who will be positively impacted by their fulfillment. We may create the next big invention, discover a life-saving intervention, or create a new art form that enables people to express their creativity in new ways. Nothing we do takes place in isolation. When we live our dreams, we become an example for others, so they, too, can have the power to follow their dreams.

Earlier, I discussed being clear about what we want, because understanding what we want is the key to unlocking our dreams. If we don't know what we want, we won't be able to tap into our desires. Once we understand what our dreams are, we must not waver from them. We must not downscale them because we're worried they may not come true.

Believe in your vision more than your reality.

To align ourselves with our biggest dreams, we must believe in them more than in our outer reality. We give too much power to the outer world to tell us where we are. We rely on the scale or on our bank accounts. Just because this is who we think we are right now doesn't mean we can't change our reflection in the next moment.

I learned this lesson from Neville Goddard.[2] He tells the story of how his teacher, Abdullah, told him to use his imagination to align with his desire to go to Barbados for Christmas. Abdullah told Neville that to align with his desire, he had to know that he already possessed it. Neville was poor at the time and couldn't afford a holiday in Barbados. Every time Neville asked Abdullah how to make his desire a reality, his teacher said, "Neville, you are in Barbados."[3] However,

Neville had doubts and became more and more worried the closer it got to Christmas. Still, he practiced going to bed each night as if he were in Barbados. When Neville asked Abdullah why his strategy wasn't working, Abdullah said, "Neville, you are in Barbados," and slammed the door in his face. When he slammed the door, he was doing what David and I talked about—getting out of his rational mind. Neville's logical reasoning mind told him that he was running out of time, that he was in New York. His heart told him he was in Barbados.

Very close to Christmas, Neville, unexpectedly, received an invitation from his brother to go to Barbados, all expenses paid.

I've used a similar strategy for things I desired, including receiving a gold medal for my master's research. I desired a gold medal because I thought it would give my work recognition. As soon as I expressed the desire, I felt myself having the gold medal and let it go. There was no question in my mind that I'd received it, even if reality was telling me I didn't. Nobody nominated me for anything. But I didn't doubt my vision. Today, I'm delighted to share that I did, indeed, receive a gold medal without doing anything on my own to acquire it.

If we have a desire, it means that desire wants to be realized within us. Our job is to believe in that dream regardless of what appears "out there." At one point, I thought I should use the following strategy to manifest my dreams: focused on my desire, wait to see it come to fruition reality, and expect to feel good. But the process is actually the reverse. We can envision our desire, feel good, and go about our day without contradicting the feeling that our desire's already been accomplished. For example, if we want to be abundant, we can imagine it in our minds, experience feelings of the abundance, and then let them go. During the day, even if we receive bills, we can love them. We can thank them for giving us the opportunity to practice who we really are and then, even if we can only pay a dollar, we can pay it with gratitude. We can imagine how we'll feel when they're paid off.

The most important thing about this form of envisioning is that we must feel it in our hearts. Once we truly tap into that feeling, it really doesn't matter if the desire shows up or not. We will feel fulfilled.

> ♥ *Heart Stretch*: *You can use numerous approaches to imagine and feel your dream coming true. You can use Dr. Joe Dispenza's meditations, Fred Dodson's PURE technique, or another approach, such as the one I outline above. The point is to get yourself out of your daily thoughts and beliefs to keep your attention on your dreams. Find what feels right for you.*

One of the keys is to avoid sabotaging our alignments with negative thinking, speaking, or acting. We must be bold. We must speak and act as if we've already received our desires. Does it mean we should go out and spend a lot of money if we're poor? No if that's going to bring us a lot of fear and vibrate us out of our beliefs. Most people who overspend do it to feel better not because they already feel abundant. But, to demonstrate our faithfulness to our desires, we can buy a nice outfit or purchase furniture for a house we want.

The most important part is retaining our vision of our dreams and not allowing ourselves to get discouraged when we don't see them become a reality. Constantly checking in on the progress of your dream only reinforces that it's not here yet. The same goes for constantly asking God/Source/Universe for what we desire. When we do this, it means we don't believe they got the message; it means we don't believe or dream is on its way or already here.

Lastly, on my journey to living my dreams, I used to talk myself out of pursuing them or downscaling them. When I stopped flip-flopping and was honest with myself about what I really wanted, I could align myself more easily.

♥ *Heart Stretch*: *Close your eyes and relax your entire body beginning from the bottom of your feet all the way to the top of your head. Breathe in and out three times to keep your attention on your body. Now focus on your heart and rest your hand there. From this place, answer these questions:*

- *How do you react when your desires don't come true right away?*
- *How do you feel when unexpected events happen that you deem negative?*
- *Are you able to get back to feeling more positive?*

We must also be willing to dream the biggest dreams we can hold in our imagination. Right now, I will share my biggest, boldest dream: I know that there are 8, 9, 10 billion people alive in this world who truly love one another. Each being on this earth is living their best lives, thriving in joy, play, health, abundance, peace and connectedness. I know they love themselves and others fully, unconditionally. I know that everyone is doing the best they can at every moment and that there's a divinity in every person I meet, even if I don't see it. I believe that this new world is alive and well. It's waiting for us to align ourselves with it.

> ♥ *Heart Stretch*: *Close your eyes and relax your entire body beginning from the bottom of your feet all the way to the top of your head. Breathe in and out three times to keep your attention on your body. Now focus on your heart and rest your hand there. From this place, answer these questions:*
>
> - *Does my vision trigger you?*
> - *Did it automatically lead you to think it's impossible?*
> - *Revisit the biggest and boldest dream you wrote down earlier. Has it changed?*

Gratitude and joy as cheat codes

Joy and gratitude are important for helping us align with the good in our lives. When my kids are having a hard time feeling motivated in school, I ask them if there's anything they're doing that could bring them joy. Of course, my question is always met with eyerolls and deadpan faces, but what I'm trying to show my children is that they always have a choice when it comes to how they feel about where they are in life. If we're always waiting for life to give us what we need to find joy, we'll never experience it. Tapping into our joy and gratitude gives us true feelings of pleasure, ease, grace, excitement, and relaxation, which arise from knowing that everything is taken care of and that our lives are what we desire them to be.

My daughter and I were on a walk, discussing our dreams. I asked her why she wasn't using her usual strategy when it came to a problem she was having.

"Most of the time, I just say what I want, and I just let it go. Then it just comes," she said,

"Does it work all the time?" I asked. But I already knew the answer.

She shrugged.

To be honest, I'm not sure she even considered using her usual manifesting strategy for the things that mattered to her.

"I've found," I said, "that when I have limiting ideas about my desires, getting myself into a general state of gratitude and joy works well because that's how I'd feel if all my dreams came true."

"Ohhhh! Is that like a cheat code?" she said.

I laughed. "Wow. I never looked at it that way, but, yes, I guess it is."

When I get myself into a state of joy and gratitude, unexpected bonuses come. One day, I was feeling joyful for no reason other than being grateful for being alive. We went out for dinner as a family, and I stopped at my favorite spa to purchase products. I was feeling so good that I entered a draw to win incredible prizes. I didn't think much about it until I found out I won the big prize: a year's worth of free facials. That alignment came from simply being in a state of ease and happiness, right where I was.

But there is a caveat: we can't lie to ourselves about where we are. We can't cheat the cheat code. We can, however, take baby steps when finding joy is too challenging. I try to find an emotion that can make me feel a little bit better than where I am. I don't do this by ignoring my emotions. At times, my thoughts tell me I feel fine, but my body and my emotions tell me the truth. Thus, I welcome all emotions with an equal amount of gratitude. I send my emotions love, which helps them relax.

I also find meditation helpful when I get too attached to my story or my identity. By focusing on that void I mentioned earlier, I get into the silence and allow myself to choose what I want to create and how I want to feel. One thing I didn't realize I'd find in meditating was the space between thoughts. At first, I couldn't meditate for five minutes; now, I relish meditating for an hour and a half or more. The space between my thoughts allows me to create space between myself and the story I created about a given situation, which allows me to begin choosing my thoughts.

One reason joy and gratitude work as cheat codes is that they allow us to let go of our striving to achieve. When we let go, we emit a signal that our wish has already been fulfilled, that we can focus our energy on something else. My dream of working in child welfare came into alignment once I let go of the fear of being unemployed and decided to focus my energy on having a great Christmas.

One of life's paradoxes is that, at times, opposite things tend to be true. Sometimes doing nothing is actually doing something. When I do nothing, my body relaxes, my mind eases, and my body can do the work of healing, repairing, resting. One of my husband's favorite sayings is "Go slow to go fast." I didn't always get what that meant, but with awareness that sometimes letting go allows answers to come to us, I realized it's true. When we let go, we receive; when we don't care, we attract. This is what David calls being in allowance, which means no longer being in a state of resistance. Letting go, however, has been one of the hardest lessons for me to learn, probably because fear played such a prominent role in my life. I feared that if I let go, everything would fall apart. Interestingly, though, when I did let go after realizing I had no other options, everything fell beautifully into place. But why wasn't my experience enough to convince me that everything would turn out right? One of the most amazing and awe-inspiring aspects of manifesting things, is that they often come when we least expect them and in the least expected way. It's delightful but also one of the most challenging aspects of releasing our dreams to God/Source/Universe. It's the not knowing how it's going to turn out that scares us.

We receive the things we don't care that much about because there's little resistance. It's almost like the Universe/Source takes the most direct path. The more we care about something or have a limiting belief about something the more resistance and fear we introduce into the expression of our desire. The more fear we have, the further away we are from aligning with our dreams. The first thing I had to learn to let go of was the "how"—how it was going to happen. My human self has a limited perspective, so when I allowed the "how" to figure itself out, it often did, in the most surprising ways. When I was too caught up in the how, I created resistance and talked myself out of some incredible desires. Now I choose to say yes to the big things that come my way and that excite me, and the how reveals itself at the perfect time.

For me, letting go also entailed letting go of the physical world. I had to let go of my extreme focus on my physical body and the reality of this world. There was a time when I worried so much about my physical body, about what the mirror was showing me, that I'd lose focus and be paralyzed in fear. When I realized that I'm more than this body, more than this existence, when I embraced my unity with the Source of all that is, I truly stepped into my own power and opened myself up to magic. I could see that only my consciousness exists, and it dictates the experiences I have. What I see out there isn't as real as I think it is.

David shared with me a strategy you may find useful. He told me to place the event on a TV screen, as if I were watching it as an objective observer. I've found this helps me not get so caught up in the drama of my life. From that space, I can observe how I'm contributing to where I am in my current reality.

This strategy has helped me realize that that the path to greatness, to joy, to our dreams isn't linear. Getting that part-time job, or contract, or whatever didn't mean the end of my dreams. I knew that the Universe/God/Source was constantly guiding me toward my greatest good, whether I was working part-time in an organization or whether I was meditating at home, releasing my fears. Whatever I needed to do to assist myself in the journey was absolutely perfect.

Epilogue

No one can grow, without outgrowing.
~ Neville Goddard

When I began this book, I thought its purpose was to change the way we think about work. I was resistant to finding employment, even temporary employment because I didn't like the way we work. My desire was to discuss how we could inject greater compassion and love into organizations and systems overtaken by dehumanizing approaches. But in the process of writing, I realized I needed to change. When I reflect on my journey, I realize it wasn't about whether I got a job. It was about the healing I needed to do in my relationship with work. The down time in my business was perfect for me to understand who I was and who I desired to be, regardless of what work currently looked like for me. I was focusing on changing my reflection in the mirror rather than myself.

Since that time, my perspective on work and my place within it has changed greatly. I now feel that my "work" here on earth isn't simply to be of service but to master myself. When I began mastering my beliefs and feelings, things started to shift. Yes, I took contracts while building my business and loved every minute of it because I realized I had the power to influence my experiences. It was about how I was showing up in my life and at work.

The chapters in this book mirror my personal growth. I had to examine all the limiting beliefs, misconceptions, erroneous perspectives, and difficult emotions I had about several challenging topics to understand what I wanted to create. Over time, the purpose of this book changed to understanding what our true purpose in life and work are. We've placed work in a little box separate from our personal lives. But every aspect of our lives is an intricate part of who we are at any moment. We have made work into this thing we do rather than a true extension of ourselves. How can we bring our whole selves to our life and what we call work? We are more than just our job, or what we do. We are more than our careers, or the value we derive from our accomplishments.

At the deepest level, I've come to realize this book is about achieving mastery over ourselves and our work. As we step into our true power as a society, and embody the essence of who we truly are, we'll begin to see our world transform.

Acknowledgments

First and foremost, to my beloved husband, David, with whom I share my struggles as well as my joys. I'm grateful to have you in my life. Thank you for all your wisdom and support. The best is yet to come for us, baby.

To my wonderful children, Milena and Enzo, who bring me such joy. I'm so lucky to be your mom. Thank you for picking me.

To my wonderful extended family, in-laws, cousins, and friends, a huge thank you. Some of you have been my biggest cheerleaders, and each one of you has given me a gift I will cherish forever. To Lisa and Steve for your incredible generosity, a big thanks. Claudia, much appreciation for being my biggest promoter and for always helping me achieve the best quality. I love and am grateful for you. And to Sarah, thanks for being my first follower, without you I'd be a lone nut.

To my beautiful sister, Jessica, who taught me compassion toward others early in my life. And to my parents, a big thanks for supporting me and liking all my posts. Mom and dad, I know that despite being worried about me, you understood my vision and supported my dream.

To my developmental editor, Christina M. Frey; my copy editor, Lesley Erickson; my format copier, Oprah Milan; and everyone involved in helping me bring this dream to life: thank you for helping me make this book the best it can be. To the amazing Laura Boyle for the beautiful cover of this book. Thank you also to Randy Peyser, Corrine Casanova, Sigrid Macdonald, and Danielle Arbuckle for your feedback on my manuscript. It was very helpful.

And lastly, to all my teachers who helped me learn through adversity and joy. I'm so grateful for everything I've learned thus far and continue to learn. You are a gift.

No man is an island . . .

~ John Donne

Notes

Chapter 1

[1] Alexander Bartik, Marianne Bertrand, Zoe Cullen, Edward Glaeser, Michael Lucac, and Christopher Stanton, "The Impact of COVID-19 on Small Business Outcomes and Expectations," *PNAS* 117, no. 30 (2020): 17656–666.

[2] Jennifer Liu, "Roughly 47 Million People Quit Their Jobs Last Year: All of This Is Uncharted Territory," CNBC.com, February 1, 2022, https://www.cnbc.com/2022/02/01/roughly-47-million-people-quit-their-job-last-year.html.

[3] Noella Ovid, "Posthaste: Almost a Quarter of Canadians Changed Jobs amid the 'Great Resignation,'" *Financial Post,* July 29, 2022, https://financialpost.com/executive/executive-summary/posthaste-almost-a-quarter-of-canadians-changed-jobs-amid-the-great-resignation.

[4] Kim Parker and Juliana Menasce Horowitz, "Majority of Workers Who Quit a Job in 2021 Cite Low Pay, No Opportunities for Advancement, Feeling Disrespected," Pew Research Center, March 9, 2022, https://www.pewresearch.org/fact-tank/2022/03/09/majority-of-workers-who-quit-a-job-in-2021-cite-low-pay-no-opportunities-for-advancement-feeling-disrespected/.

[5] Jennifer Liu, "Why Does Work Feel So Dysfunctional Right Now? A Psychologist, Labor Expert and CEO Weigh In," CNBC.com, September 26, 2022, https://www.cnbc.com/2022/09/26/why-does-work-feel-so-dysfunctional-right-now-experts-weigh-in.html.

[6] Donald Sull, Charles Sull, and Ben Zweig, "Toxic Culture Is Driving the Great Resignation," *MIT Sloan Management Review,* January 11, 2022, https://sloanreview.mit.edu/article/toxic-culture-is-driving-the-great-resignation/.

[7] Emma Charlton, "Four Things Workers Want Implemented by Their Bosses Post-Pandemic," *World Economic Forum,* May 7, 2021, https://www.weforum.org/agenda/2021/05/employers-pandemic-covid-19-mental-health/.

[8] Lisa First-Willis, "Inspiration Is the Key to Employee Retention in Today's Complex Work Environment," *Clean Link,* February 2023, Inspiration Is the Key to Employee Retention in Today's Complex Work Environment (cleanlink.com).

[9] Monica Worline and Jane E. Dutton, *Awakening Compassion at Work: The Quiet Power That Elevates People and Organizations* (Oakland, CA: Berrett-Koehler 2017).

[10] Ashley Stahl, "What's Really Happening with Quiet Quitting?" *Forbes,* November 2, 2022,

https://www.forbes.com/sites/ashleystahl/2022/11/02/whats-really-happening-with-quiet-quitting/?sh=61a837eb2ab1.

[11] Liz Kislik, "What Do Newer Generations of Employees Want, And Can Your Business Adjust?" *Forbes* (January 28, 2022), https://www.forbes.com/sites/lizkislik/2022/01/28/what-do-newer-generations-of-employees-want-and-can-your-business-adjust/?sh=47d244112ee0; Katie Kuehner-Hebert, "Millennials Want Job Stability, Gen Z Wants Passion," *Benefits Pro,* November 21, 2017, https://www.benefitspro.com/2017/11/21/millennials-want-job-stability-gen-z-wants-passion/?slreturn=20230108103634; and Lauren Loftus, "Generation Un-grind: Now That Hustle Culture Has Crashed and Burnt Us All Out, How Are Young People Viewing Their Future Work?" *Santa Clara Magazine,* December 5, 2022, https://magazine.scu.edu/magazines/fall-2022/generation-un-grind/.

[12] Dianna Labrien, "8 Reasons Millennials Seem to Be Lazy at Work," *Life Hack,* (January 2023, https://www.lifehack.org/articles/work/8-reasons-millennials-seem-lazy-work.html; and Terry Nguyen, "Gen Z Does Not Dream of Labor," Vox.com, April 22, 2022, https://www.vox.com/the-highlight/22977663/gen-z-antiwork-capitalism.

[13] Rob Carrick, "Why Young Adults Can't Afford Houses: Hard Work Got You More in the Past Than It Does Now," *Globe and Mail,* January 19, 2022, https://www.theglobeandmail.com/investing/personal-finance/young-money/article-why-young-adults-cant-afford-houses-hard-work-got-you-more-in-the-past/.

[14] Carolyn Ockels, Steve King, and Gene Zaino, "Workers Don't Feel Like a 9-to-5 Job Is a Safe Bet Anymore," *HBR,* March 23, 2022, https://hbr.org/2022/03/workers-dont-feel-like-a-9-to-5-job-is-a-safe-bet-anymore.

[15] Ashley Capott and Sofia Pitt, "Google, Microsoft, Amazon and Other Tech Companies Have Laid off More Than 70,000 Employees in the Last Year," CNBC, January 20, 2023, https://www.cnbc.com/2023/01/18/tech-layoffs-microsoft-amazon-meta-others-have-cut-more-than-60000.html.

[16] Amanda Perelli, "How Much Influencers Get Paid on Instagram, TikTok, and YouTube," *Business Insider,* December 20, 2022, https://www.businessinsider.com/how-much-influencers-get-paid-on-instagram-tiktok-and-youtube-2021-7.

[17] Syed Rufaid, "Emergence of Social Media, a Growth in Career Opportunities," *Higher Education Review,* January 2023, https://www.thehighereducationreview.com/magazine/emergence-of-social-media-a-growth-in-career-opportunities-DHKD816153861.html.

[18] Paul Sullivan, "How the Pandemic Has Changed Attitudes toward Wealth," *New York Times,*

May 21, 2022, https://www.nytimes.com/2021/05/21/your-money/wealth-attitudes-pandemic.html.

[19] Jordan Turner, "Employees Seek Personal Value and Purpose at Work: Be Prepared to Deliver," Gartner.com, January 13, 2022, https://www.gartner.com/en/articles/employees-seek-personal-value-and-purpose-at-work-be-prepared-to-deliver.

Chapter 2

[1] Jeremy Seabrook, "The Language of Labouring Reveals Its Tortured Roots," *Guardian,* January 14, 2013, https://www.theguardian.com/commentisfree/2013/jan/14/language-labouring-reveals-tortured-roots1.

[2] Josephine Joly and Luke Hurst, "Four-Day Week: Which Countries Have Embraced It and How's It Going So Far?" *Euronews Next,* January 24, 2023, https://www.euronews.com/next/2022/12/19/the-four-day-week-which-countries-have-embraced-it-and-how-s-it-going-so-far#:~:text=Iceland%3A%20One%20of%20the%20leaders,part%20in%20the%20test%20phase.

Chapter 3

[1] Maxwell Maltz, *Psycho-Cybernetics: A New Way to Get More Living out of Life* (Englewood Cliffs, NJ: Prentice Hall, 1960).

Chapter 4

[1] Rhonda Byrne, *The Secret* (New York: Beyond Words, 2006); and Gabrielle Bernstein, *The Universe Has Your Back* (Carlsbad, CA: Hay House, 2016).

[2] David Cox, "Canada's Forgotten Universal Basic Income Experiment," *BBC News,* June 24, 2020, https://www.bbc.com/worklife/article/20200624-canadas-forgotten-universal-basic-income-experiment.

[3] Ken Honda, *Happy Money: The Japanese Art of Making Peace with Your Money* (New York: Gallery Books: 2019).

[4] Chris Germer and Kristen Neff, *Teaching the Mindful Self-Compassion Program: A Guide for Professionals* (New York: Guildford Press: 2019).

Chapter 5

[1] Jennifer Goetz and Emiliana Simon-Thomas, "The Landscape of Compassion: Definitions and Scientific Approaches," in *The Oxford Handbook of Compassion Science,* ed. Emma Seppala, Emiliana Simon-Thomas, Stephanie Brown, Monica Worline, Daryl Cameron, and James Doty (Oxford: Oxford University Press, 2017), 3–15.

[2] Olga Klimecki and Tania Singer, "The Compassionate Brain," in Seppala et al., *The Oxford Handbook of Compassion Science*, 109–20; Olga Klimecki and Tania Singer, "Empathic Distress Fatigue Rather Than Compassion Fatigue? Integrating Findings from Empathy Research in Psychology and Social Neuroscience," in *Pathological Altruism,* ed. Barbara Oakley, Ariel Knafo, Guruprasad Madhavan, and David Sloan Wilson (Oxford: Oxford University Press, 2012), 368–83; and Olga Klimecki, Susanne Leiberg, Matthieu Ricard, and Tania Singer, "Differential Patterns of Functional Brain Plasticity after Compassion and Empathy Training," *Social and Cognitive Affective Neuroscience* 9 (2014): 873–79.

[3] Paul Gilbert, "Compassion Focused Therapy, Pt. 1–4" (paper presentation for CCARE, Stanford University, Palo Alto, CA, April 2013).

[4] Luis Ospino, "The Myth of Narcissus: Being Vain in Greek Mythology," Greek Reporter.com, September 6, 2022, https://greekreporter.com/2022/09/06/narcissus-greek-mythology/#:~:text=The%20word%20%E2%80%9Cnarcissistic%E2%80%9D%20is%20often,was%20reflected%20in%20the%20water.

Chapter 6

[1] Emma Seppala, Timothy Rossomando, and James R. Doty, "Social Connection and Compassion: Important Predictors of Health and Well-Being," *Social Research* 80, no. 2 (2013): 411–30, https://www.jstor.org/stable/24385608.

[2] Louise Hay, *Mirror Work: 21 Days to Heal Your Life* (Carlsbad, CA: Hay House, 2016).

[3] B.T. Spalding, *Life and Teaching of the Masters of the Far East,* vols. 1–6 (Marina Del Ray, CA: DeVorss Publications, 1924).

Chapter 7

[1] Neale Donald Walsh, *Conversations with God: An Uncommon Dialogue* (New York: Tarcher Perigee, 1995).

[2] Tony McAleer, *The Cure for Hate: A Former White Supremacist's Journey from Violent Extremism to Radical Compassion* (Vancouver: Arsenal Pulp Press, 2019), 188.

[3] Thomas King, *All My Relations: An Anthology of Contemporary Canadian Native Fiction* (Toronto: McClelland and Stewart, 1990).

[4] R. Kronick and C. Rousseau, "Rights, Compassion and Invisible Children: A Critical Discourse Analysis of the Parliamentary Debates on the Mandatory Detention of Migrant Children in Canada," *Journal of Refugee Studies* 28, no. 4 (2015): 544–69.

[5] Pema Chödrön, *The Places That Scare You: A Guide to Fearlessness in Difficult Times* (Boston: Shambhala, 2001).

Chapter 8

[1] Robert Rosenthal and Lenore Jacobson, "Pygmalion in the Classroom," *Urban Review* 13 (1968): 16–20, https://doi.org/10.1007/BF02322211.

[2] Neville Goddard, "How to Manifest Your Desires," *Radio Lectures* (1948). https://www.law-of-attraction-haven.com/support-files/how-to-manifest-your-desires-neville-goddard.pdf

[3] Valerie Kaur, *See No Stranger: A Memoir and Manifesto of Revolutionary Love* (New York: One World, 2020), 148.

[4] Chris Germer and Kristen Neff, *Teaching the Mindful Self-Compassion Program: A Guide for Professionals* (New York: Guildford Press, 2019).

Chapter 9

[1] Liz Dufour, "Mom Wants to Help Teen Involved in Her Son's Death," Cincinati.com, November 14, 2017, https://www.cincinnati.com/videos/news/2017/11/14/mom-wants-help-teen-involved-her-sons-death/107685336/.

Chapter 10

[1] Centre for Addictions and Mental Health, "Trauma," https://moodle8.camhx.ca/moodle/mod/book/view.php?id=189&chapterid=435.

[2] Joe Dispenza, *Becoming Supernatural: How Common People Are Doing The Uncommon* (Carlsbad, CA: Hay House, 2017).
[3] Fred Dodson, *Parallel Universes of Self* (Fred Dodson), 2006.

[4] Susan Pollak, *Self-Compassion for Parents: Nurture Your Child by Caring for Yourself* (New York: Guildford Press, 2019).

[5] Joe Dispenza, *Becoming Supernatural: How Common People Are Doing The Uncommon* (Carlsbad, CA: Hay House, 2017).

Chapter 11

[1] Robert Kiyosaki, *Rich Dad Poor Dad: What the Rich Teach Their Kids about Money That the Poor and Middle Class Do Not!* (Scottsdale, AZ: Plata Publishing, 1997).

Chapter 12

[1] C.D. Cameron and B.K. Payne, "Escaping Affect: How Motivated Emotion Regulation Creates Insensitivity to Mass Suffering," *Journal of Personality and Social Psychology* 100 (2011): 1–15.

[2] Paul Gilbert, "Compassion Focused Therapy, Pt. 1–4" (paper presentation for CCARE, Stanford University, Palo Alto, CA, April 2013).

[3] Ely Garfinkle, "Shame: The Hidden Resistance," *Canadian Journal of Pyschoanalysis* 20 (2012): 44–69.

[4] Brene Brown, "The Power of Vulnerability," Ted Talk, December 2010,

https://www.ted.com/talks/brene_brown_the_power_of_vulnerability/comments.

[5] Marianne Williamson, *A Return to Love*: *Reflections on the Principles of a Course in Miracles* (New York: HarperCollins, 1992).

Chapter 13

[1] Derek Sivers, "How to Start a Movement," TED Talks, March 2014, https://www.ted.com/talks/derek_sivers_how_to_start_a_movement.

[2] Tolle Eckhart, *Stillness Speaks* (Vancouver: Namaste, 2003).

Chapter 14

[1] bell hooks, in conversation with Maya Angelou, *Shambala Sun,* January 1998, http://www.hartford-hwp.com/archives/45a/249.html.

[2] Nadia Cameron, "How Brands Are Exhibiting Kindness in Leadership and Organisational Action," CMO, August 30, 2022, https://www.cmo.com.au/article/701051/how-brands-exhibiting-kindness-leadership-organisational-action/; and Blake Morgan, "Why a Corporate Culture of 'Kindness' Is Great for Your Brand," Forbes.com, April 27, 2015, https://www.forbes.com/sites/blakemorgan/2015/04/27/why-a-corporate-culture-of-kindness-is-great-for-your-brand/?sh=790b6f50681d.

Chapter 16

[1] Thich Nhat Hanh, "Letter after Hearing of Dr. Martin Luther King, Jr.'s Assassination," April 5, 1968, Plum Village, https://plumvillage.org/about/thich-nhat-hanh/letters/letter-after-hearing-of-dr-martin-luther-king-jr-s-assassination/.

[2] The Sacred Hawaiian Way, "Kahuna Hale Kealohalani Makua," http://www.thesacredhawaiianway.com/kahuna-hale-makua.html.

[3] Daryl Davis, *Klandestine Relationships: A Black Man's Odyssey in the Ku Klux Klan* (Far Hills, NJ: New Horizon Press, 1998).

Chapter 17

[1] Louise Hay, "Louise Hay", accessed April 19, 2023. https://www.louisehay.com/101-best-louise-hay-positive-affirmations/

[2] Neville Goddard, *How to Manifest Your Desires: Rare Lectures by Neville Goddard,* 1948, https://www.law-of-attraction-haven.com/support-files/how-to-manifest-your-desires-neville-goddard.pdf.

[3] Ibid., "Lecture 3: Thinking Fourth Dimensionally."

About the Author

Gissele Taraba was born in Lima Peru and immigrated to Canada when she was 10 years of age. She has two amazing children, and is married to her life partner David. She also has a dog named Baron, who is her third child. Gissele has completed two Masters Degrees, one in Health Research Methodology and another one in Social Work. Gissele has been in the workplace for over 20 years and worked in a number of not for profits. She has also received numerous business certificates including a leadership certificate from the Rotman School of Management, University of Toronto. Gissele has also received training on mindfulness, and compassion and self-compassion and loves to be of service. She is the host of the *Love and Compassion Podcast with Gissele* and her dream is to help people remember that love and compassion have the power to heal our lives and our world!

If you love this book, please don't hesitate to leave an Amazon review! Leaving a review will help expand the book's reach.

o If you want to work with Gissele or David, email them at info@maitricentre.com

o To listen to their podcast, *The Love and Compassion Podcast with Gissele,* you can find it here: https://maitricentre.com/blog/ and here https://www.youtube.com/channel/UC0WhWcp4jlTPuwE2 _6AVs_Q

o Follow them on social media:
  ▪ Facebook: https://www.facebook.com/maitricentre1/
  ▪ Instagram: https://www.instagram.com/maitricentre1
  ▪ Twitter: https://twitter.com/maitricentre/
  ▪ YouTube: https://www.youtube.com/channel/UC0WhWcp4jlTPu wE2_6AVs_Q
  ▪ LinkedIn: https://www.linkedin.com/in/gissele-damiani-taraba-msc-msw-12995091/
  ▪ TikTok: https://www.tiktok.com/@maitricentre?is_from_webapp= 1&sender_device=pc

www.ingramcontent.com/pod-product-compliance
Lightning Source LLC
Chambersburg PA
CBHW020536030426
42337CB00013B/873